When asked why he carved, Michelangelo replied, "I saw an angel in the marble and carved until I set him free." Fr. Herman Falke also carves and paints with the eyes of his faith to free his viewers' consciousness to view truth and beauty by using a new lens to explore a shared humanity.

Fr. Peter McKenna, SCJ – Ministry Director of Becoming Neighbours

"Thanks very much for sharing this with me. In fact a very inspiring life... Charles."

Charles Taylor – Professor/Philosopher (McGill University)

"Fr. Falke's book is a worthy addition to your list."

James Carroll – major American, Catholic author

"Father Falke's amazing life is immersed in Blessed Creativity. His passion for humanity and his unwavering faith manifested in a sublime portfolio of work."

Judi M. Young – President, Sculptors Society of Canada

"First, I found Fr. Falke's sculptures intricate and unorthodox in form but always well-crafted. On further investigation coupled with his own back story, I saw more details surface that told a rich story displaying real human sensibility and traditional, Christian spiritual values. He sculpts a piece of wood into a 3D figure filled with character and attitude. Truly the work of an inspirational artist and storyteller."

Alex Tirabasso – Artist/Engraver, Royal Canadian Mint

Father Falke turns the everyday into art.

Wendy-Ann Clarke – The Catholic Register

Other Works by the Author

From Uganda with Love (1980)

Sculptures of The Passion (1996)

Spirit & Life in Sculpture (1998)

Scripture Sculptures in Wood and Clay (2004)

Sculpted Swan Songs (2008)

p.s. There's more (2009)

And This is What He Taught (2011)

(Versions in English, French, Dutch)

A CELEBRATION OF LIFE IN ART

Fr. Herman Falke S.C.J.

SCULPTOR, PAINTER, TEACHER, PRIEST

Edited by Michael J. Walsh

A CELEBRATION OF LIFE IN ART

Fr. Herman Falke S.C.J.

SCULPTOR, PAINTER, TEACHER, PRIEST

Edited by Michael J. Walsh

Library and Archives Canada Cataloguing in Publication

Title: A celebration of life in art / Herman Falke.
Names: Falke, H. (Herman), author, artist.

Identifiers: Canadiana (print) 20210378980 | Canadiana (ebook) 20210379014 | ISBN 9781771615969 (softcover) | ISBN 9781771615976 (PDF) | ISBN 9781771615983 (EPUB) | ISBN 9781771615990 (Kindle)

Subjects: LCSH: Falke, H. (Herman) | LCSH: Sculptors—Canada—Biography. | LCSH: Sculpture, Canadian—20th century. | LCSH: Catholic Church—Canada—Clergy—Biography. | LCGFT: Autobiographies.
Classification: LCC NB249.F35 A2 2021 | DDC 730.92—dc23

Published by Mosaic Press, Oakville, Ontario, Canada, 2022.

Mosaic Press, Publishers
© Copyright Herman Falke 2022
Printed and bound in Canada.

Editor: Michael J. Walsh
Designed by Andrea Tempesta • www.flickr.com/photos/andreatempesta

ONTARIO ARTS COUNCIL
CONSEIL DES ARTS DE L'ONTARIO
an Ontario government agency
un organisme du gouvernement de l'Ontario

Funded by the Government of Canada
Financé par le gouvernement du Canada

Canada

We acknowledge the Ontario Arts Council
for their support of our publishing program

MOSAIC PRESS
1252 Speers Road, Units 1 & 2, Oakville, Ontario, L6L 5N9
(905) 825-2130 • info@mosaic-press.com
www.mosaic-press.com

CONTENTS

A Celebration of Life in Art

When a few months ago I asked Fr. Herman Falke what he considered to be his major contribution to art, he responded without a pause: "I am one of the few artists today engaged in religious art." As this book shows, that is how he wishes to be remembered. I was first introduced to Herman's engagement with art when I was a teenager. On Sunday afternoons, Herman would gather some students to show slides of art in a small room at one of the cottages at the Belvoir Estates in Delaware, Ontario, which a few years earlier had been transformed into a seminary. For a number of Sundays in 1954, Herman, who at the time was completing his own theological studies at St. Peter's Seminary in London, Ontario, introduced us to paintings and sculptures of the Renaissance. It was my initiation to the appreciation of art in its various forms. Herman must have been 25 years old at the time. Much of my life the coincidence of living in the same community house with Herman meant living with his art—the strong and the weaker ones. The walls on the three floors of the house where I live are covered with his paintings and his sculptures. There is no escaping from them. About 25% of the pieces have overt religious themes, many derived from biblical accounts. For a good portion of his life, Herman worked out his religious perspectives in pieces of art: paintings, sculptures in fieldstone, wood, and ceramics. But depicting a biblical story in paintings and sculptures does not necessarily make these pieces religious art. For that something more is required. To be religious art – the paintings and the sculpture—must be more than a mere memory of a biblical story or a flat imitation. In the current secular context, with the cultural loss of the memory of these biblical stories, such paintings and sculptures are often today no longer recognized and have lost their meaning. To be religious art it has to have an inherent drawing power. It must stop you in your tracks. It must make you pause—even for a brief moment—and invoke reflection. Standing before the object of art, the spectator will want to understand what it is about this piece that evoked a feeling of wonderment, unease, partial recognition or a vague intimation of a surplus. Religious art should transcend its materials. Something more is at stake in the viewer that is not immediately available. Obviously not all of Herman's pieces fall under the category of religious art. And if beauty is found in the eyes of the beholder, there are a few pieces that qualify as religious for me. Two biblical images stand out for me. One is the depiction of Mary's greeting of Elizabeth (on page 95). Both women intimately grasp each other's body where such a deep tale of life for others is taking place. There is something being communicated to the beholder in the very intimacy of these two women: there is a deep carnal knowledge making the divine almost tangible. The second sculpture was the touching of the side of Jesus by Thomas after the resurrection. The sculpture is not as powerful as the intrusive painting of Caravaggio of Thomas exploring very explicitly with intense curiosity the wound in the side of Jesus. Jesus is directing the hand of Thomas right into the wound. Herman's sculpture is less carnal than Caravaggio's and Thomas does not look directly at the wound towards which Jesus is leading him. He looks away in our direction leaving us to figure out what he is feeling and thinking. He seems in touch with something that stupefies him and which is turning his life upside down. We, the viewers, are left to ponder what it is that so astonishes Thomas.

What has always struck me about Herman's painting's and sculptures is the awkwardness of the human figures. At one time I asked him about this feature of his work. He replied a figure or a painting ought never to be so natural that you do not give it a second look. So, in his paintings, but especially in his sculptures, there is frequently something awry in the imaging. The emotions expressed on the faces are out of sync or out of proportion, excessive in relation to the scene. Often the faces are primitive, filled with emotion. And bodies are contorted. There is no clear message conveyed by the contortions. Only they make you pause. It leaves the viewer pensive. He or she is drawn back to the total image and wonders what to make of the struggles and the awkwardness of the personages in the sculpture or painting.

The story of Herman's life is here told in all simplicity. The story seeks to make sense of a life-time of art. Like all stories—particularly in our time—the life-story of Herman is not linear. Although there seems to be a continuity inasmuch as most of his life he saw himself as an artist, the influences of his origins, his movement from one continent to another, his shifting career in teaching and the call to ministry in a number of parishes, and his years of retirement, the changes in culture from the 1930s to 2021 affected him as everyone else, except as an artist he needed to physically portray it. If one reads his story with his images you can see and feel, how these shifts in time and culture touched his spirit and became represented in his art. His life in art is perhaps one way of reading your own way through this time.

John van den Hengel scj

Anyone growing into his teens will become aware of how precious a human life is, and what potential lies just beyond the horizon. The joy of doing well in group sports or the excitement of finding fulfilment in a hobby like bicycling or fishing or painting can give anyone a specific pleasure in life.

Serious engagement in a hobby will not be free from set-backs and disappointments at times, (just as in real life). There are times of hardships and even disasters. Consider Hitler, Idi Amin, and the disintegration of organized religion after Vatican II.

All of the above have tempered the sanity of my otherwise pretty stable celebration of life.

Friends of mine, a young Dutch farming couple, bought a farm with a big old farmhouse near Stratford, Ontario around 1960. In the attic they found a stack of old Time magazines from throughout the 1940's. They let me go through them and in one I found a yellowed advertisement, picturing three guys and a sad dog sitting around an iron woodstove singing their hearts out. The pictures of their sweethearts on the back wall suggested that their "*hurtin' songs*" contained clouds in the skies covering up their love lives.

I took several liberties recreating the same picture, notably, with the removal of a row of liquor bottles prominently displayed in the foreground. I like this painting because it pleasantly combines the laughter and the tears with the laughter dominating. And even if tears are shed, it's still a celebration of life. You don't need whiskey for that. Life interweaves happy events with sad ones. You can just let life pass you by, or you can use it or learn from it to celebrate it in art, music or drama As the Good Book states in PS. 90: "Our lifespan is seventy or eighty years for those who are strong. Yet mostly they bring us trouble and sorrow, making us come to terms with the shortness of our life, so that we may gain wisdom of heart.

CHAPTER 1
DUTCH ROOTS

Planning to write the biography of an artist, an author searches high and low to establish whether or not an artist's talents are in his genes. My Father was a High School teacher. His subjects were Geography and French. He was not creative nor artistic, but he loved singing in the parish choir. He was colour blind, unable to distinguish green from blue.

My Mother had only a grade six education, which was the tops for any girl in the 1890's. She was the only daughter of a grain miller who built and maintained his own windmill. He had 50 beehives and an orchard of some 30 fruit trees.

He carved wooden shoes (clogs) for family and friends and wove baskets from willows that he grew. With fieldstones he built the front gate of his garden and somehow chiseled a huge stone into a round ball and placed it on top of the gate. If my Mother and I had any artistic bent, it was from him. Of course, a century ago it was not called art, but rather things beautifully made, a joy to see and touch.

My Dad, true teacher that he was, had two left hands, literally. Once my Mother said to him, "I'll be out shopping for a short while. Will you put the ironing board back in the cellar?"

"Oh sure". Twelve wooden steps would lead to a cement floor. A half an hour later when my Mother came back home, she found him unconscious on the floor, although the pipe in his mouth was still lit. He had broken the wrist of his right arm. Then he trained himself to write left-handed with chalk on the blackboard and resumed his teaching routine.

Dad had been a corporal in the Dutch army during WW1 and for one long winter he had been isolated with 10 other soldiers on a very small island with only two farms located in the North Sea. All they had to eat that winter was mutton and potatoes and more mutton and potatoes daily. Mother was never allowed to serve mutton in our home after the war.

Dad got a teaching position in a new Catholic High School and married my Mother, the miller's daughter in 1920.

They quickly started a family and recorded it in a thick photo album.

Harry was the first boy born, and he features large in the family photo album, even with a bare-bottom pose on a fluffy pillow.

Ben was the second boy born two years later. He also features well in the photo album. Casper was the third boy born two years later. He doesn't show up at all as a baby in the album. Then finally two years later, in 1928, I was born.

"Not another boy!" my parents must have sighed. I remained invisible as a baby. My first appearance was in a photo taken impulsively when I was about four years old. I have my Dad's pipe in my mouth, and there is a goat next to me whose existence I do not recall.

In 1934 when I was six years old and in Grade One, my mother was expecting her fifth child, this time (Thank God!) a girl. The photo album started to make up for the slack time of the previous eight years and my parents had a new larger house built.

Our complete family in our back yard around 1938. I am the smallest boy to the right of my father.

The Falke family lived in the new house for 33 years when my parents sold it to a local storekeeper for ten times its original cost. That's inflation for you! It was a convenient house, not really luxurious. The living room had a double-glass door that opened to a veranda and then to an attractive garden that was half orchard and half vegetable garden. It was my Mother's pride and joy.

In one corner of the living room was a piano, and hanging above it a violin with bow, although I had never heard my Dad playing either one. He said that his four-years of military service killed whatever instrumental skills he had. He stuck to his singing.

There were three pieces, of what one might call pieces of art, hanging on the walls of our new home. The most fascinating piece was a large canal scene in Amsterdam with a well-known church steeple in the middle background. Years later when my aging parents hoped to leave one important memory of the past to each of their children, I was expecting that Amsterdam canal scene, but

Amsterdam by evening

CHAPTER 1: DUTCH ROOTS

my brother Ben had already earmarked it. Then my parents suggested. I should take an antique Frisian clock. But I couldn't see myself dragging a big clock across the ocean to a Community House already full of clocks. I ended up with a few Frisian copper pots that I might use in some future still life painting class at my school.

In our front room (or salon) there was another equally large Amsterdam landscape scene with a flower market and nearby canal. Obviously Amsterdam meant a great deal to my Dad. After all he had studied there for his teachers' training.

Amsterdam is the most typical Dutch city, cherished by all Hollanders. In May 1940, when Hitler's armies invaded Holland, they bombed and burned Rotterdam, that archrival of Hamburg. Then they proclaimed an ultimatum.

"Unless you surrender, we will do the same with Amsterdam."

Holland surrendered.

My own painting showed the core of old Amsterdam where two main canals came together. All the narrow buildings were the factory homes of merchant families who warehoused spices from the Far East including peppers, nutmeg, chocolate and coffee that had been processed and stored. Transport was by canal boats, and each house had a tackle at the top of the façade to swing the exotic products to any of the large windows or gates. For two centuries Amsterdam was the wealthiest city in the world.

On the top floor of one of these factory homes the family of Ann Frank tried to survive extermination in 1942-3. That location is still a major tourist attraction.

The third, an even larger painting in our new home was one commissioned by my Mother. It pictured meticulously the homestead and windmill of grandfather. Even the front gate and the rounded rock on top of it were present. But my parents were only moderately satisfied with this piece done by a local artist, and hung it above the staircase in the hall, practically on the second floor.

At school I was a good student and always placed first or second in my class. My favourite subject was Geography and the only present I remember was a world atlas from my Father when he bought himself a new updated one. The wonder of our wide world fascinated me.

Something else that attracted me early was religion. We lived only a five minute walk from the

village church, and the bells were rung ten minutes before each Mass. Almost every day before the early 7 o'clock Mass I heard those bells, jumped out of bed, threw some water over my face and raced for the church. I was just in time for the *"Introibo ad altare Dei",* the first words of the Mass. One gray morning as I was racing down the stairs for church, my Mother called out:
"Herman, can you get me my socks. They are drying along the mantelpiece in the living room."
"Yes Mom." I dashed through the room and ripped the socks away with one hand. But down came a Delft-blue vase that had held the tips of the socks and it fell to the floor in smithereens!
I was not punished for my carelessness. My parents understood the accident and appreciated my daily routine. They were good Catholics. My Father was a member of the Third Order of St. Francis and wore a scapular medal under his clothes at night. My Mother had two aunts who were cloistered nuns, and a brother who was a Franciscan priest and had been a Missionary in Brazil for 24 years In hindsight I wouldn't be surprised if it was my Father who had planted a pamphlet in my room written by Rector van den Hengel. It described the attractions of a vocation to the priesthood, and ended with a novena asking God to give you such a vocation. I started that novena in earnest. My parents were pleased that I had chosen to go to a Junior Seminary run by the Priests of the Sacred Heart. The son of one of our neighbours was there already, five years ahead of me. He was Frans ten Bosch, who in 1964 became a martyr in Wamba, Congo.
In April 1941 at the ripe age of 12, I went by train for five hours to the other side of Holland beside the seashore. The main subjects of our studies were two dead languages, Latin and ancient Greek. The Seminary was spacious enough and housed 200 students along with teachers and staff. It was surrounded by sports fields and vegetable gardens. But the occupying German Army were jealously eyeing us and ordered us out by mid-1942. For the next two years we scrambled around in four groups to four different locations with one in an abandoned brewery, two in local parish halls, and one in a castle with a moat and drawbridge. I was assigned to a parish hall which also included the clubhouse of the boy scouts. It involved a lot of make-do and improvising.
Here are two illustrations.
For teenagers the one rationed pair of poor shoes a year was insufficient. Gradually we started to wear wooden shoes (clogs). When the villagers were coming out of their houses on Wednesday

and Saturday afternoon 30 of us came clack-clacking over the cobblestones on our regular hikes. The Nazis and their security police were always wary of underground resistance and sabotage. Therefore they started rounding up men between 16 and 45 who could not produce an official work permit. Half a dozen of our students were 16 or over and every evening, after seven they went separately or in twos to an old castle that had been converted into a long-term care center. There they spent their nights in an attic.

When the school year ended in July 1944, the Normandy invasion was in full swing. We went home not knowing what the future would bring, but certainly not a return to our parish hall and club house.

I was barely home when the Allies broke through, liberated Paris and pushed north towards Holland, hoping to cross the bridges around Arnhem and then swing into Germany. It failed. Two German tank divisions were waiting for them, *"One Bridge Too Far,"* and the war on the West Front came to a halt from August 1944 till March 1945.

However, the fighting continued above our heads. Every night tight squadrons of heavily loaded bombers flew over us to bomb a designated German industrial city or military concentration. With searchlights the Germans tried to spot the planes, and when they caught one in the light, they directed the cannons on it. In a desperate attempt to evade, the plane would release all its bombs and thus regain some manoeuverability. Three such loads fell near our village which was very close to the German border. One unloading hit the soggy playgrounds of our elementary boys school, some 800 meters from our house. Mud splashed over one side of it. With some old bricks and cement we built a shelter in our garden and covered it with sods. For five months almost every night when we heard the familiar drone in the sky, we each grabbed a house blanket and spent a few hours underground, just like the people in London, England, as we learned later.

Even on clear days the R.A.F. started to gain control over all our movements on the ground. At first there were dogfights with German Heinkels, but the Germans were overextended and were running short of equipment and trained personnel. During the day, German transportation hid under the trees and in barns. Nothing could be seen on the roads or railways.

One day Dad came home from a funeral service at the church pale as a sheet and with muddied trousers.

As was customary, a horse-drawn hearse would lead the mourners to the cemetery just outside the village. An R.A.F. plane spotted movements and out of the blue sky plunged down and strafed both the hearse and horse. All the people walking behind the hearse jumped into ditches or behind tree trunks. With dry gallows humour my Dad commented, "If the man in the coffin hadn't been dead, he's dead now."

In hindsight I feel guilty that as a young teenager I found it all exciting during the day the dogfights and planes falling from the sky followed often by parachutes opening, and during the night the searchlights and the suspense lighting up the night sky. Deeper concerns and worries were troubling my parents. I made myself useful to our family and the refugees that were assigned to our house by collecting firewood which had become the only thing available for cooking and heating. I also collected extra food from friendly farmers nearby, who would allow us some milk, eggs or grain weekly. Food was never an issue in an agricultural region in contrast to the heavily populated western part of Holland where the people were approaching the edge of starvation on a diet of turnips and tulip bulbs. To discourage an Allied invasion, the Germans had inundated the central part of the country. People from cities in the west like Amsterdam and Rotterdam could no longer gather some extra food in our area of plenty. Desperation seeing victory slip away and Hitler's propaganda about the superiority of the German race contributed to the Germans abandoning justice. Occupied countries could be exploited and pilfered with impunity.

The few Jews who were living in nearby towns, including the piano teacher who used to come weekly to teach my two oldest brothers, simply disappeared. Rumours about what was happening in Dachau and other concentration camps became stronger and more specific. My mother's cousin, a policeman, who unbeknownst to us worked with the underground resistance, was suddenly picked up in our village and transported to a local concentration camp. We wouldn't have known it, but at the last moment he gave his bicycle to a boy and said,

"Here bring this to the Falkes".

After the war his remains were found in a mass grave alongside 200 other resistance men.

Holocaust

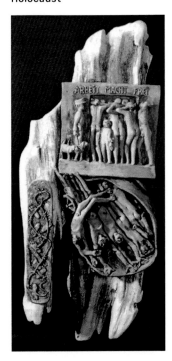

In the heat of the outrage, I made the first composition in somber grey ceramic, and embodied it into a large piece of driftwood.
—
Detail of above sculpture.

The bicycle came in handy, because the German soldiers were stealing them at random as their only safe transportation. We lost one that way so we buried two in our garden and kept a miserable old one in view to avoid any suspicion that we were hiding something. Indeed one day two German soldiers came to our door, "Do you have any bicycles? The army needs them."

We showed them our poor specimen and they sneered at it. "Is that all you have?"

"Well, the German Police stole the rest." Indignantly they shouted back, "That's not stealing. That's organizing for the army and for victory."

A German victory was still a reality not eliminated from any German propaganda. Hitler promised a new weapon that would quickly bring the British to their knees. It was the horror of Germany's V2 rockets, capable of travelling far beyond the speed of sound with a heavy load of bombs.

London became the target throughout the month of November 1944. And since the Allies had by then liberated the whole coastline of France and Belgium up to Antwerp, the large launching pads had to be constructed along the Dutch coastal area that was simply depopulated, including much of The Hague, the capital city of Holland. Tens of thousands were notified to go somewhere else by a certain date in early October. Our house, was ordered to take in an elderly lady from The Hague, and a 19 year old girl from the emptied city of Arnhem whose family had been spread out over our neighbourhood. No ifs and buts.

Then all men between 16 and 50 (I was 16 and my Father 48) had to come to the Town Hall on a specific Monday in September to be divided into work groups. In our village nobody showed up. My Dad and I went into hiding at a farm where the two of us played a lot of chess and spent uncomfortable nights trying to sleep in a hay barn.

The Germans rounded up ten men from anywhere in the village and announced that unless the men of the village turned up, those ten will be executed and another ten will be rounded up. It had already happened in a few towns such as Apeldoorn. Over the weekend our Pastor and the Reformed Minister decided that we should show up. The next Monday morning eleven hundred men stood in front of the Town Hall, including my Dad and me.

My Dad, because he was a teacher, became part of the small administration group and was assigned an "intellectual" job: drawing up Fever Charts for the hospital. After a week he realized he could do this job much better at home as long as he produced the needed quantity of charts. They let him do that. The main purpose for rounding up the male population was to forestall the formation of a local Dutch resistance.

I was assigned to one of several groups to construct trenches along the River Rhine and its contributories, and to dig man-holes along main roads about ten meters apart. We were quartered in several schools which had been closed. From our backyard I dug up one of our bicycles since it was now protected by my work permit. Also because we went home on weekends, we loaded up on hardboiled eggs and home-made bread to supplement our simple army chow.

Our guards were older soldiers, grandfathers really, who never did us any harm, except once nearly. Our assignment for making those V-shaped trenches required three different jobs: the actual digging of the trenches six feet deep; the woodwork to strengthen the sides and the weaving of pine branches to contain the soil behind the woodwork. Instinctively we did as little work as we could get away with.

One bright Friday afternoon, I and two former classmates were assigned to gather pine branches in a forest about 30 minutes away. When each of us had collected enough branches for an impressive bundle we lay down on the moss and chewed the cud until half an hour's walk brought us back to the trenches 15 minutes before closing time at five o clock. Therefore, when we came out to the open ground near the river we saw nobody except two guards, who told us that an hour earlier everyone had left for home because they had completed their section. "But you, lazy bums must see the police first."

Dreadful! What could happen to us?

We made our story sound innocent, but as acceptable as possible, and waited for the verdict. The officer looked us over from head to toe and said: "You three deserve to spend some time in one of our camps or correction centres." The three of us immediately thought of concentration camps and started to sob. The policeman must have realized how young we were and snapped. "Get out quickly. *"Gehen Sie heraus schnell."*

We continued our work on the useless trenches along the Rhine around Emmerich in the N.W. corner of Germany, an almost two hour, bike ride from my Dutch hometown. Occasionally an R.A.F. spotter flew over us, and we were ready to jump for safety into our own trenches. But they never came down to strafe us.

They must have realized that we were forced labour from an occupied nation. To the south of us a large group of captured Russian soldiers were doing the same work on the trenches.

Only once did I become involved in an actual strafing and it was a frightening experience which I can never forget. A group of us were biking back to our quarters. We passed two local women walking their bikes with some heavy bags on them. Then a nice German army car drove by with two officers in it and a soldier sitting on the hood, scanning the sky. Suddenly an increasingly loud roar blasted down on us from above. The three Germans were the first to jump for safety before the *ratatat* of bullets tore through the car that sagged down on the tarmac and caught fire. I didn't see it all, because intuitively I dropped my bike and dove into the nearest manhole. I stayed as down as possible against the expected return of the plane half a minute later from the opposite direction for another strafing. One of the German women was crying hysterically. A bullet had hit her leg above the knee. I saw a lot of blood before I grabbed my bike and rode in a daze to our quarters.

Back home my Mother had spoken with our town mayor (who had gotten his position because he was a collaborator, a Quisling) and told him that I was a Seminarian and therefore, legally free from labour. The mayor must have started to realize that the writing was on the wall for further

German control and he agreed with my Mother. He wrote a comical permit for me to continue my Latin studies at home. *"Dominus vobiscum!"*

I quickly resumed the collecting of firewood and piano practising daily. I didn't even bury my bicycle. With my new permit I had more freedom to collect extra food.

My bicycle brought me to the second part of my artistic DNA, after the playing of music that is. Two miles from our house was a large castle that had been converted into a reformatory school for minor infractions. I happened to meet its art teacher and showed an interest in his work. He modelled clay and then with plaster of Paris constructed a piece mold around the figure with a moist clay to get a perfect negative in plaster. "Would you like to have some clay to try out?" I got a box with maybe five kilos of damp clay that still had some plaster chips from the teacher in it and I became hooked. Over the winter I spent considerable time modelling angels for Christmas, as well as horses. I never thought that this pastime would ever turn into more than a minor hobby, but it did. It changed my life.

In the winter of 1944-5 my lost school year turned out to be a blessing because I became an adolescent and learned to cooperate with others; to overcome crises, and I learned the joy of simple together-ness in the long evening curfews around a candle to conserve our restricted kilowatts. Our stories and laughter at the expense of Hitler and the Nazis could have put us all in a concentration camp. This critical time not only brought me to the beginning of a new hobby in ceramic sculpture, but also turned into a year of serious piano playing. Since our Jewish piano teacher had mysteriously disappeared, my Dad found another teacher at least as good. She was a young married woman with a one-year old baby, living in a cramped 2nd Floor apartment.

I always wondered how they got the piano upstairs. I went there each Friday afternoon as long as I could because almost immediately after the War she emigrated to New Zealand where she had relatives. I made a good progress with her and by August 1945 I could scrape through a few easy Chopin waltzes.

On Holy Saturday in 1945 our village was liberated without any damage. The last Germans had simply bicycled east to their homeland on our bicycles! Dad had just returned from church with new Holy Water when Canadian tanks rolled in over the cobble stones of the main street. Free at last after five years. Canadians soldiers handed out three things: cigarettes, chocolate and white bread. Who could have imagined bleached white bread? A miracle.

By August 1945 the school year in our Seminary by the seashore started anew. Travelling was still awkward. The first part of the journey was on a local truck. In Arnhem I could only cross the Rhine by boat underneath the ruins of that "one bridge too far". Then on the train mostly in a cattle car. For three years I plowed through so much Latin and Greek that there was no room for any art except Gregorian chant, and two pianos.

No wonder there are so few artists among the clergy except for musicians and writers.

There was one personal happening that would become a great influence on my personal life. The priest who was usually playing the organ for Mass and Benediction was looking for a musically aware, volunteer to turn the pages for him and pull stops on winks. I volunteered, but sometime later this priest was frequently absent for Benediction in the evening.

Instead of letting 200 Seminarians sing *a cappella*, I gave them a one-fingered accompaniment. During the supper that followed I received much teasing. So I decided to learn playing three or four standard songs and the next time when I had to fill in, nobody noticed the substitution. I had made myself into an organist at the ripe age of 19. In the Novitiate that followed and in the Major Seminary, after that I was simply the Organist.

One thing that stands out in those last three Dutch years, even more than music, was my return to sculpting with clay. Studying full time philosophy for two complete years was hard on me. I was in danger of losing my capacity for poetry and originality. Everything had to be unassailably logical. It bored me to tears to stand at my desk for hours on end, memorizing soulless philosophical definitions in Latin.

Luckily I found in the attic a bucket of clay abandoned by an artistic student who had recently left religious life. Eagerly I started using my spare time from October 1949 on to get back to ceramic sculpture. There was a brickyard within walking distance where my bucket of clay had come from. I started to find out that those brickyard people were happy to bake sculptures by local artists placing them on the edges with the bricks sticking out a bit. For them it was finally something exciting.

St. Andrew bringing up boy with food   St. Francis

CHAPTER 1: DUTCH ROOTS

After a few testing pieces I became ambitious. I had over two months left before Christmas. The Community had an old chipped Nativity set with the edges showing the white plaster of Paris. With my clay I modelled the first six figures of the Nativity set: two sheep, one shepherd and three kings. With these baked in the brickyard, I went to the bursar: "If you buy me a paint box, I will finish a whole Nativity set for the chapel by Christmas." It became my first real success.

In 1950 I concocted an even more ambitious project that would take me more than a year to complete. Our major Seminary housed 65 S.C.Js, 50 students, eight professors, and seven Brothers as support staff. When they entered religious life, each had chosen a specific patron saint. For instance, I chose St. John Bosco, canonized in 1936. The project I came up with was to model a sculpture of their patron saint for all 65 confreres and have it on their breakfast table on the feast day of that saint. It took me a full year and I learned a lot. Many saints look similar whether they carry a crucifix, a book, or a church. I must have created a fair number of duds, but also several that were deeply appreciated. For instance, an elderly professor had St. Ambrose as his patron saint. He looked after a few beehives in the garden, and there he placed my sculpture of St. Ambrose, because he was the patron saint of beekeepers. St. Ambrose was described in his biography preaching so sweetly that bees flocked to his lips.

Some 30 years later when I revisited Holland, one of or our S.C.J. Brothers came up to me and said, "Oh Father Falke, I still have the sculpture you made for me in the Seminary."

My early stint creating sculptures of saints by the dozen has taught me to avoid them if possible. Most of them are too static, two uninspiring. Years later I did carve a few upon request. As long as I could substitute the traditional crucifix on their chest or a book (bible or constitutions) on their arm, I might comply. But I would select something more humane to set them apart from us sinners. The examples given here demonstrate that St. Andrew is neatly described in John 6: 8-9 as having that human touch looking for a practical solution to feeding the hungry crowd of listeners. He has spotted a boy who has some bread and fish that Jesus might use. For me that touch of attentiveness is enough to set St. Andrew's sculpture apart from the run-of-the-mill.

St Francis of Assisi is perhaps our most popular saint, not so much because of all the pious things he did, but more because of his love of all God's creation and the conservation of our world. The sculpture selects the total confidence of a deer and a dove and St. Francis' care for them.

The ceramic sculpture of St. Joan of Arc is as far away from the traditional depiction of saints as I care to go. I modelled Joan as a full-blown teenager, hardened by several military campaigns and months of horse riding and now facing martyrdom with confidence in God.

Still art had nothing to do with my moving to Canada. That "honour" must go to music, which will become clear in chapter two.

Joan of Arc, the Maiden of Orleans, to be burned at the stake

CHAPTER 2
ART SQUEEZED IN

Hitler's dictatorship with all the cruelties and injustices it entailed was an evil that increased over the five years of occupation, but kept hurting people after the liberation in April 1945, with the necessity of rebuilding roads and bridges, and some whole towns like Rotterdam and Arnhem with few resources or money. American help using the Marshall Plan came years later. But ironically interwoven with the hardships of the aftermath of WW2 something positive grew.

The Canadians were the liberators across Holland and they were received as heroes. Friendships were formed naturally and with their return to Canada they brought along some 6000 war brides. Already before 1950, the Dutch and Canadian governments put their heads together and devised a large-scale subsidized project to bring young, Dutch farmers to Canada. Holland had a huge surplus of young farmers and a shortage of farmland, while Canada had a huge surplus of neglected and underused farmland and a shortage of willing farmers. Between 1948 and 1956, a quarter of a million Dutch immigrants accepted the free transport by boat and settled in Canada with over half of them moving straight to the farms, half of which were in Southern Ontario. Most of these farms were relatively small and mixed, and therefore, similar to what these new arrivals had left behind in Holland.

The Bishops of Southern Ontario were worried when rural parishes found it difficult to accommodate so many Dutch-speaking newcomers at once, and they investigated where in Holland there would be priests available. Just then we S.C.J.*ers* were experiencing peak growth in Holland with over 800 members, while for ten years nobody could be sent to our traditional mission territories of Indonesia, Finland and Congo due to the War and its aftermath.

When the Dutch S.C.J. Province promised the Ontario Bishops' Conference that they would send one or two priests to each diocese that needed them for work among immigrants, they added one request that we be allowed to establish our own Junior Seminary for continuity. The Bishops' Conference agreed with one counter request that this Seminary should be open to candidates from any diocese and religious congregation.

It was agreed, and with a loan from our American S.C.J.'s, we bought a 300 acre estate in Delaware near London, Ontario that had a large mansion on it. In the scramble to secure a proper staff for the Seminary, a request was sent in 1951 to the major Seminary in Holland for two or three Seminarians in final vows to come to Canada and finish their studies there. One of them had to have musical abilities to handle a Seminary choir.

There were 50 Seminarians at the right stage of accepting this challenge. But I knew that if I would put my name down. I would be selected, and so it was. When people ask me, "What brought you to Canada?" I must answer, "Music made me come to Canada."

Soon in the early 1950's a dozen Dutch priests arrived to work among the immigrants. Each bishop from London to Ottawa entrusted to each of us a parish so that we would have some financial support, and a base to work from. The work consisted mostly of listening patiently to the stories of loneliness far out on a farm, and to provide comfort and assurance, and real help when needed. Youth clubs were organized, even soccer clubs and choirs, marriage preparation and a few credit unions.

Whole sections of rural SW Ontario were served regularly by all our Dutch priests for confessions. The 1950's and 1960's was still the time when most Catholics felt that going to Confession regularly was part and parcel of a Catholic life.

Confession line-up

The eight--male staff at the Delaware Seminary fanned out every weekend to provide assistance, using one car with two priests to serve parishes west of London, and another car with four priests to the east serving Aylmer, Tillsonburg, Delhi and Langton in the real tobacco belt. Half the parishioners there were Flemish, Dutch, German, and other nationalities. The mainly Irish pastors were happy to have us come on weekends, leaving the three hours of steady confessions on Saturday evenings to us, while they watched "Hockey Night in Canada" and "My Pet Juliette".

Welkom

Meantime, while this ministry among new immigrants was taking shape, I finished my studies and was ordained a priest in September 1954 at St. Peter's Seminary in London Ontario. No family was able to attend; no pictures were allowed to be taken. However, when I returned to Holland for my "First Mass" the whole village turned up to welcome me.

Back in Canada I started teaching in our Junior Seminary while taking courses at Western University, London, for a B.A., to qualify for the Teachers College. Somehow in between all this, I managed to take one or two courses each year in sculpture and landscape painting. When you're young you think you can do everything. That's partly true which I found out in my Delaware years, and later in Africa. The Senator Little Estate in Delaware could barely house our staff and 25 students. It was expanded with a nice complex that could accommodate over 80 students. At my request they constructed into the new building a comfortable art room right above the stage of the gym. That's where I did a lot of my art and taught art. But I had to overcome two difficulties. First I needed a kiln to fire my ceramic sculptures. With a huge mortgage hanging over the new building, I had promised my superiors that I would assume all expenses of running the art program from the sale of my art. A suitable kiln would cost $900 How to get that much money? I found a way. For $900 I painted a complete set of 14 Stations of the Cross for the church of a priest and friend of mine. A few years later when my Dad got his teacher's pension, I invited my parents for a summer vacation in Canada, and of course, I asked them to pose with my first major art commission outside the old church.

My parents with two of my 14 Stations of the Cross

My second difficulty lay with the Principal of the Seminary (school), which was a boarding school. To him art was something frivolous, unsuitable for priests or seminarians. They should stick to studying and perhaps practicing Gregorian chant at which he was lousy.

At one time I started to outline and paint a mural of the *Canticle of the Sun* with St. Francis on an empty wall in a classroom. The principal walked by, stopped and stared at my work for half a minute before saying, "Is it difficult for you to cover that up again?"

From the start of my teaching he made it clear that there was no room for art teaching in the schedule, and for two reasons.

Art was a subject without substance in his humble opinion, and secondly the ten students interested in art were in four different grades and could not be blocked together without upsetting the whole schedule.

That second argument made sense with our small student body. Still I was determined to somehow squeeze art in for these candidates to the priesthood. It was no wonder that there were so few priest artists. We came to a compromise. I should teach art on the weekends, since I was usually free from participating in the assistance to parishes in the tobacco belt because I had to play the organ and train the choir for the Gregorian chant of our Sunday liturgy. Most of the Saturday evenings during the school year I taught art for a select group of students. Actually that nearly undetermined timeslot had the great advantage of allowing the students to really dig into a project and get their paints or clay out, so to say.

I might suggest a ceramic project by doing a hand, or a face, or a statue. Or I would set up a still life less complicated than the one shown here and leave it up for one or two more weekends. However, when I had my Saturday evening art class, while the other students were playing ping pong or pool, or more likely watching ,"Hockey Night in Canada". Sometimes a student would storm into the gym and shout up to the art room: "a fight, a fight!". In ten seconds my art room was nearly emptied as all wanted to see the hockey fight on T.V.

On visiting Sundays most of the students wanted their parents to see the art room. I was looking forward to that also, because I sold many of my art pieces to them. One sale I remember clearly. Just at the edge of the village of Delaware there was an ugly dumping place of car wrecks. The first

Still life: Eve with apple

By way of exception I set up for myself a still life with a vaguely spiritual theme. It was probably the tall Indonesian woodcarving in the back that triggered this, because it seemed to suggest male dominance. An antique bible that is somehow weighing down on a contrite Eve, and an apple with one bite taken out, supplement a somewhat wishy-washy religious idea.

snowstorm of one winter covered most of the rusty iron. I made a pencil sketch of it and then at home I made a large 36-inch wide painting of it on the rough side of a Masonite board. Into my art room walked the parents of one of the boys from Owen Sound. They oohed over that painting. To them it was sheer poetry, for they were the managers of a similar junkyard. They bought the piece, and I was actually glad to get rid of it. I don't even have a photo of it.

Another time a man walked into my art room, glanced around for a few seconds, and stared at only one still life painting of a few bottles on a table cloth. "Now that's what I consider art", he said. "You can really see the different types of glass." It takes all sorts of people to make this world interesting.

Around 1965 things in the Catholic Church changed dramatically. Old rules and practices were finally being questioned in Vatican II. Democracy in the Church and the role of women were finally talked about tactfully, though still not really openly. The conservative Vatican hierarchy was powerful enough to block any movement to modern progress.

One third of the clergy left the priesthood and most of them got quickly married. Vocations to life-long celibacy and the priesthood evaporated. Our Junior Seminary in Delaware became a convenient dumping ground for divorced/separated parents:

"Let's get our boy with those priests. Maybe he'll learn some discipline."

I was 37 years old and had no desire to get stuck in this kind of pointless existence, comfortable though it was, and convenient for doing art. There was little challenge in it: my biggest, daytime class, Grade 10, had ten students, and my smallest, Grade 13, had three.

At the end of the school year of 1966 the staff had three days of serious discussions whether or not we should continue the school, and the unanimous conclusion we reached was that we should not waste the time of eight priests any further on an institution that had lost its purpose. Each one had a choice to go into ministry or parish work, or upgrade himself at a University. My Provincial Superior left me free to look around for something in line with my special abilities.

The Canadian University Service Overseas (CUSO) brought me in contact with a large group of French-Canadian teaching Brothers (F.I.C. *Fréres de l'Instruction Chrétienne)* who had establish several of the leading Secondary Schools across East Africa. They were searching for a priest who was qualified to teach a subject at St. Mary's College in Uganda, and at the same time would function as their chaplain.

Perfect! It was absolutely cut out for me.

I was ready for a new adventure.

CHAPTER 3
ENLIGHTENED ON THE DARK CONTINENT

Flying on four propellers from Rome to Entebbe Uganda in one stretch can be a weird experience. We followed the Italian coast from one volcano to the next. Especially the huge Mt. Etna on Sicily was impressive with its smoke plume. Then after the narrow strip of thin vegetation along the Libyan coastline there was sand, nothing but sand.

At sunrise we landed at Entebbe on a narrow peninsula in Lake Victoria, the source of the Nile. Three Brothers welcomed me and drove me the six kilometers to St. Mary's College.

"What will you have for breakfast? Cornflakes or bacon and eggs?"

Later their Brother Superior explained to me, "We live and have our meals very much like in Canada. Our real sacrifice living here is that we must accept that it is Africans who tell us what to do. And that is very hard, because quite often their decisions seem illogical to us.

During the months before I arrived in Uganda early August 1966, I often wondered how much I would become involved in the traditional tasks of the Church such as religious instruction, baptisms, etc. Soon it became clear to me that I had come too late for that. More than 70% of Ugandan villagers were firm Christians for the second or third generation, and the local clergy was taking over from the aging white missionaries, even from the bishops. I baptized not a single person during my African years. My single task was teaching school subjects at the College level.

It took me ten days early in August to get acquainted with my textbooks for teaching English, my art program, and with the whole college campus, which consisted of some 80 separate buildings, one of which was my art room.

The school was located near the equator in a rain forest belt on the shore of Lake Victoria. As a result, another old hobby of mine, collecting butterflies, blossomed into a major distraction. Collecting insects day after day, season after season, enabled me to send and sell thousands of butterflies and beetles all over the Western world, and to enlarge the collection of the Entomology Research Institute at the Experimental Farm in Ottawa with over 25,000 insects. They paid me 7 cents per pinned-up specimen, the Scrooges! "Make sure you collect a lot of butterflies for our display cases", our biology teacher in Delaware had urged me. In tropical Africa there are easily ten times as many different species as in Canada in the best seasons, and in Africa they were around all year. Finally I could relax and I stepped out of my room, armed with a butterfly net.

CHAPTER 3: ENLIGHTENED ON THE DARK CONTINENT

A Ugandan fellow teacher asked me from his front yard, "Where are you going?"

I said, "To the forest down there at the shore of Lake Victoria".

He said, "Oh you can't", and added wide-eyed, "Snakes!"

From childhood on, those bare-footed African children have been taught, "Stay out of the forest". On my first days in the forest, I was probably overly-cautious. Later on I remained prudent and always on the alert. In my six years in Africa, with on average five fieldtrips a week, I encountered less than two dozen snakes, likely half of them harmless, such as small boas.

Actually I was more concerned with safari ants. They travel in almost endless columns on the paths for more than ten yards on both sides with ants that are looking for anything edible, including me. That's why I kept wearing a woollen barrier in the form of socks.

Daily I had to teach one period of English to two Grade 2 classes (Gr.10 in N. America), and the rest of the day Art, basically painting. Art was a compulsory subject in Grades 1 and 2 and optional later. All my English students were also taking art with me. That created a strong bond with about 55 students, and it encouraged them to be open with me. This helped me to learn about their family and tribal life. Other white outsiders, except Church and medical personnel, wouldn't get much more than superficial knowledge of what makes our Africans tick. Especially volunteer teachers from England showed a tendency to remain British and uninvolved. Two newcomers from England began asking questions while they were having their regular drink after work and expressed their joy in the good life they were having in Uganda: "What a wonderful place to live in! Too bad there are so many black people living here." 99% no less.

I started teaching mid-August 1966, and as early as Monday, September 12th, "I was struck by the spontaneity of my students' work." I wrote in my diary, "Suddenly as I was marking essays, the idea came to me to write a book—a book of essays written by my students here, and introduced and woven together by me according to a range of topics. And, for the time being I'll just copy by hand the more significant ones of these essays."

Unfortunately for me, there were no copying machines of any kind. So it was a time-consuming routine. Here are two of these student essays that demonstrate how precious a treasure I collected.

Test for Manhood

When a young man among our people wants to get married, he must undergo a test for manhood, an interesting ceremony called "*sharro.*" It goes like this. The boy who wants to marry tells the village chief so that this chief will prepare everything. He tells his people to come and watch; he chooses the best man in the village who knows how to beat and whip; he also builds a shelter for the young girls who want to be married.

Then the day arrives, and everybody goes to the place of the "*sharro.*" The young man stands in the middle with his hands holding a pole that is fixed seven feet above the ground. The spectators sit or stand around, leaving a way open for the marriageable girls who come from the shelter with their bodies gleaming with oil from head to toes.

Finally the man who is going to whip comes to the center with a bundle of whips. Drummers start beating a quick rhythm, and the whip-man starts dancing in circles around the young man. Then he takes out one whip, and *zooooo-mu*, it snaps around the waist of the young man. For some community reason the whip-man may put a certain medicine on his whips so that the first blows make the young man mad. He will run away and lose his chance. But if a person perseveres through the customary flogging and stays until the whip-man gets tired, the girls will come out of their shelter, and the successful suitor may choose one of them as his wife.

Simon Kirumira, S.2 A.

The following note is an attempt of mine to put several essays on the same topic in a wider context. Can we claim to be independent if in exchange for our colonial masters we find ourselves burdened with a dictator, and an ignorant one at that who does not know the ABC of running a country?" Another source that will remain unnamed wrote the following essay.

Happy To Be A Ugandan?

A few years ago life in Uganda was enjoyable; nowadays many Ugandans pity themselves that they were born Ugandans as all the good things have vanished. There is no longer freedom, everybody's life is at stake, and everybody can expect torture and death at any moment. Day after day decrees are signed limiting people's joy of life, and there is no opposition, no protest. Isn't it sad that people have even come to wish that the Colonial rule should have stayed for several more years? Outsiders refer to Uganda as "a living hell," and they are not far wrong. But even if we wish to leave in search of a life in freedom, we are unable to do so because we are native Ugandans with no other country to call our home.

All we can do now is to encourage ourselves to stick it out. Although we are suffering now, time will come when our present nightmare will be history. Meanwhile we regret having to stay here instead of living in another country where we might be poor but safe.

December 1973.

I called the book *From Uganda with Love*. The arrangement of the chapters should make it clear what I intended to learn. The first chapters deal with general topics such as their families, their villages, their schooling, and their holidays.

The book was published in 1980 in the United States, and was used in several High Schools where current events were part of their teaching schedule. It sold out and I made some money from it. Here is a critique of the book from a Canadian magazine, *The Catholic Register*.

> The book consists of letters and paintings which reflect African life during a decade of transition when Idi Amin was attempting to shame and subdue this fine country. It is also a very unusual and authentic description of this Africa seen through the eyes of young black students.
>
> **Explosive Content**
> The book is really explosive in its content, and Father Falke is both critical and bitter about the whites who go about trying to bring Western culture to what he considers a beautiful and fecund country. One learns a lot, nevertheless, from reading these essays about everyday life in this part of Africa—family ties and city life, celebrations and holidays, customs, relations to sex and marriage, and the increasing influence of Western culture. The book is both timely and provocative and the illustrations, which are mostly by the author, are very revealing.
> I found this book extremely fascinating but I am left with the impression that the author might have a great deal to say that he has not said. The reason for this I do not know, but the essays and stories of the students do in fact reveal far more of what life in Uganda is really like than any other book I have read and believe readers will share my opinion.

Here's another critique by an American magazine:

> To lovers of Africa, and Uganda in particular, and also to anyone who enjoys reading about other people, this book will bring a few hours of pleasant learning.
>
> The book also gives a lot of information on traditions, mores and habits of several Uganda tribes. It gives a positive image of the country known as the Pearl of Africa, which Idi Amin Dada has tarnished with violence.
>
> Fr. Falke, a native of Holland, gave six years of his life as a teacher of fine arts at one of the best high schools of Uganda, St. Mary's College Kisubi, run by the Brothers of Christian Instruction.
>
> The originality of his book is to depict Ugandan traditional customs on marriage, bride-price, death, etc. Through essays as well as paintings, many subjects are covered in a realistic way, by students who live those traditions. Some of the traditions are changing, in some cases to the regret of the students; in other cases with their strong approval. Whatever happens to Uganda, the quality of the students is reassuring.
>
> Fr. Falke completes their work with his own analysis which is impressive for a man who only spent six years, and all of that in a school.

I would say, it depends so much on how you spend six years teaching in a school. By putting a great deal of your energy to deeply investigating African life? Or by dreaming of getting to your British pub?

Uganda's climate is fairly even throughout the year. Therefore, I used the start of our three regular holidays of a month each, to go camping with a few students in one of three cool mountain regions, to do some butterfly collecting or some painting, and enjoy contact with the local people in evenings around their fires, using and abusing all of my 100 Swahili words and expressions.

Butterflies

My own greatest relaxation was collecting butterflies and beetles in the cool tropical forests and mountains. God must have had an inordinate love of insects. While, to our knowledge, he created only one human species, he created nearly a million species of butterflies and moths, and some 300,000 species of beetles.

My students also loved these refreshing camping and collecting trips, and for one extra reason: for nearly a week, they would be free from that back-breaking work of weeding the crop; and around 1973-4, they would have a week of tasty food (as the economic collapse had brought about shortages of sugar, bread, canned goods, and even salt). Although it was only fair for them to work for their parents, because these people often had to sacrifice as much as a third of their total annual income to support one of their children in their secondary education. My students were always totally ready when I called on them at their homes to take them along by car for our safari into the western regions.

I found this Muhavura area ideal for painting, even though I had to put up with the daily rain showers. The Muhavura range consists of four volcanos, 13,000 ft high. It forms the border between Uganda and Rwanda, and is the habitat of chimpanzees.

The foothills are cultivated for crops because the volcanic soil is very fertile. Above that is the bamboo forest where the rainclouds swirl around most of the time.

I put down my easel and started sketching the upper two two-thirds of the composition on paper. All the children of the area came crowding around and watched me carefully. They pointed out to each other the details they recognized. When I had more or less finished painting the upper two-thirds, I moved my easel 180 degrees and started filling in the bottom part with the homestead of a few of the children. A sense of awe came over my young spectators. They started calling their parents to share their indignation at my audacity for rearranging the location of their living quarters. Probably the most valuable enlightenment I received from my allotted years in Africa was "a question of how to teach art."

Ironically, it was something British rather than African.

In North America the art program in Teachers' College is basically the teaching of a bag of tricks, and perhaps some life drawing that is largely, left up to the individual teacher. The British method, which is employed in all the former British colonies in Africa and the Indian sub-continent, is much more regulated. It aims at making the art students proficient in three things: still life, nature painting, and imaginative composition.

-still life will teach them to observe objects and surfaces.

-nature painting will teach them to observe the world around them with the moods of nature.

-imaginative composition focusing on human involvement in this environment of nature and objects.

Imaginary composition is the peak of the art program. It brings together all the elements of observation under the discipline of balanced composition while at the same time allowing the artist the freedom of personal imagination.

I enjoyed teaching art in this disciplined framework, and I adopted it eagerly in my own approach to art. My first two years of painting in Africa were basically landscape painting with the occasional still life or a portrait. My last two years were more and more aiming at imaginative composition. Of course, it helped that by then I was more intimately familiar with real African life.

Painting class: Uganda

To do a nature painting takes one day or rarely two.

To paint a still life may take 3-5 days.

To plot an intricate imaginative painting may take 2-3 weeks.

I loved celebrating African life in my own distanced artistic fashion using all these elements.

My art room was a simple barn-like building with a cracked concrete floor and corrugated iron sheets for the ceiling. Half the time I let my students paint outside unless wind or rain made it inconvenient. When it rained hard on those corrugated sheets, I couldn't hear myself talk. Two students stood at each double-sided folding easels. Some of the better works I put up for display. When a student was finished he would place his painting on a low desk in the centre of the room so that I could store the work away apart from the next class. Each week I had my 200 students twice a week for a double or triple period.

For the final exams my senior students both at O and A level had to do all three paintings. One year, I recall, the instructions for the still life were to have an old basket on a table, and flowing out of it were several fish. The sealed envelope stated on the outside that I could open it earlier so that I could buy something on time in the market. The fish. The nature painting demanded a front-leafed plant out in the open. I had my students set up their easels in our banana garden.

By the end of each school year I would receive an officially sealed package with prescribed imaginative topics, of which each of my senior art students had to select one, and then prepare himself to paint it on an assigned afternoon. In 1968 a tough topic captured my imagination: "On the rough paths between the villages we noticed families on seemingly inexplicable errands...." I did three versions of it.

In one version, "we" is the shepherd boy and his goats. In the other version, "we" are the two women grinding millet. Their questioning looks accentuate the mysteriousness of the travellers. Imaginative composition was somewhat more complicated than the other two, and was therefore allowed to be a pre-sketch with charcoal from the kitchen fireplace. We spent some intense but pleasant days on them ahead of the exam. The students had a choice between 3-5 topics, and this already predetermined their capability.

All the paintings for the final exams were bundled up and sent for marking to London England, and in later years to Nairobi Kenya. Our school always ranked first or second in the five years I supervised. In all humility I must say that it was a success story. The main reason was that I was exceptionally connected with my students. Also I felt myself challenged by this new system of handling art teaching, and I led my students often by doing the assignment myself first or alongside them. On Saturday morning I always had a hard time persuading one or two students to come along

African townspeople watching a Masai family pass by (16"x24")

Mysterious travellers (18"x36")

My mother looks like an elephant

with me on painting trips in the nearby villages. For the students, Saturday was laundry day. All the bushes on the college campus were festooned with drying washings. But for me a student who spoke the local language of Luganda was most necessary to communicate with the villages and obtain their permission to interfere with their privacy for a few hours.

"How could I refuse a priest who might have to bury me in the near future", a woman told me. I gave her a piece of chocolate, exotic for her. She was pleased.

For some pages I have explained how the British method of teaching painting, together with my increasing understanding of African life had brought me to the peak of creativity in painting. Now I almost feel obliged to present here an anthology of my best African work: one still life, three portraits, four nature paintings, namely landscapes without people, and the rest imaginative compositions.

Local musical instruments

Hollowed tree sections with cowhide stretched over them while still fresh make the three drums. The bent harp with its snakeskin bottom and ivory handle compensates for the big drums, and links up the composition, as does the leopard skin below it.

Tanzanian girls shopping

What attracted me most doing this painting was the variety of clothes and baskets. In contrast to the stately dress of Baganda women, Tanzanian women dress more casually. It consists of three rectangular pieces of bright cloth, one around their hips, the next over their breasts, and the last one over their heads and shoulders. I noticed that when they are working in their fields, they wear only the one over their hips, but when a white man approaches, they grab for more.

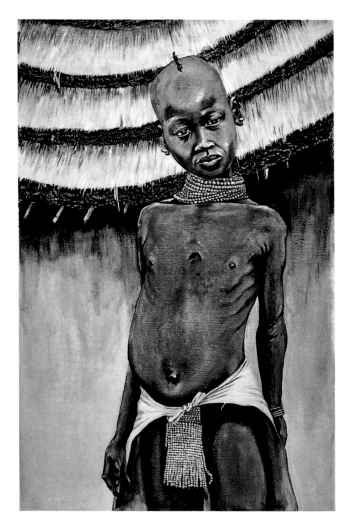

Karamojong girl

This girl belongs to the most primitive tribe of Uganda related to the Masai in Kenya. The men go completely naked even when going to church. "Why should we wear western trousers. We are proud to show off our genitals". In 1973 Amin felt that those naked Karamojong were a blemish on the image of Uganda. He sent an army detachment to force them to wear trousers. Six were shot, and the tribe started wearing trousers when they had to come near the main road.

Model posing on rug (Right)
Veronica (Below)

It's no wonder that in a poor developing country many teen-agers ran short with their school fees. They sought help es-pecially among the white school staff. There came to my door a young woman with a sturdy full body who was willing to pose if I helped her. She needed fees to complete her fourth

year of studies. She wanted to be-come a police woman.

Veronica was different. She some-times came to visit St. Mary's College where her brother, whose school fees I paid, was a student. She visited me in my room and admired some of my paintings on display. Then she timidly asked, "May I pose for you?" Here is the result which took two sessions. Her body showed magnificently the structure of her bones and muscles. A treat for an artist. She never asked for money. I guess she posed as a thank-you for supporting her brother, and also she simply liked the experience of seeing herself as an artist's model.

There is a Murchison National Park in Uganda where Lake Albert empties into the Nile River. When I first visited it in 1966 there were 5000 elephants there. When I last visited it in 1973, there were only 20 jittery elephants left. The rest slaughtered for their ivory by soldiers who got Amin's permission as a Christmas bonus. There used to be signs along the entrances to the Park: "Elephants have the Right of Way". Maybe they are sold as souvenirs.

The Great Rift Valley that starts with the Jordan River and the Dead Sea, extends south through the Red Sea and the long string of lakes in East Africa. In Uganda it forms a stretch of hot dry grassland not very good for people, but perfect for herds of game animals. Trees are sparse and cactus-like. Anything else that stick out on the plain are termite mounds.

When I came through Holland with my roll of paintings from Uganda, I showed them proudly to my family on the first evening. They all agreed that I should keep all sixty together, maybe for a future

The Ruenzori Mountains

CHAPTER 3: ENLIGHTENED ON THE DARK CONTINENT

Zebras

Elephants

The Muhavura Mountains

exhibition. Then as the evening wore on, my oldest brother said, "Let me have just this one painting". Then my sister asked the same for an African portrait. Finally my parents asked specifically for the zebras. It stayed on their wall for the next twenty years. Sixty minus three is fifty-seven, and I hadn't even crossed the Atlantic.

The transition from the low Rift Valley to the Ruenzori range is sudden. Up to this point you can travel by car or motorbike, but from here on it was on foot. The snow-capped Ruenzoris are 24,000 feet high. I used to camp on this very spot with one or two of my students and spend the evening with the owner of the compound in the foreground bartering about the fees for two porters to carry our camping equipment and food up to 8000 feet, and return four days later to carry the stuff down again.

Africans do not fence their property, but here it's necessary as a protection against wild animals from the Rift Valley below, like elephants and buffaloes. They could destroy an entire garden in less than an hour.

The other mountainous region I loved to paint was the Muhavura range with its four volcanoes, which I have already described. This compound is in the foothills of that range.

This whole region is old, black volcanic soil, very fertile and receiving copious rain. Every square yard is used to raise any crop, any kind of vegetables, cabbages, peas, beans, potatoes, bananas. A good percentage of the dense population is Tutsi refugees from across the mountains. Actually from there they apparently reconquered their homeland, Rwanda.

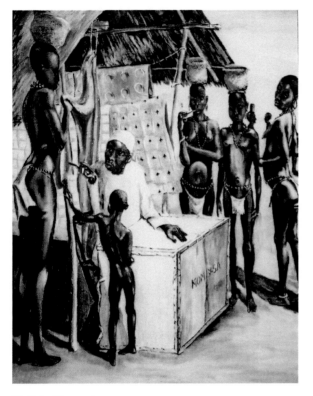

Cloth by the yard

If they wanted to dress up, the local women might buy cloth by the yard in the market. The first merchants came from India. Coming from an unnatural environment that sheltered celibate seminarians and priests from any contact with women, and even just looking at women was material for Confession, I couldn't help but notice immediately how shapely African women were in contrast to the men. These women were constantly working deep-bent in their gardens, and consequently their bodies developed more pronounced structures. Instinctively I preferred to paint imaginative compositions that displayed those attractive female features. Very likely I was overcompensating for what I had been religiously trained to avoid and overlook during my years of training. No wonder that during my first few months in Uganda I felt that African life was embarrassingly public and for all to see. People lived outdoors all day and used their huts or small mudhouses only for shelter during the nights and when it rained. Soon my embarrassment turned into fascination and then into a desire to record it in paintings. I was hooked. I paid attention to their rituals and customs. I noticed their contentment with very simple things and their care of their children with hands-off discipline.

All of it was constantly in plain view and I absorbed it greedily.

Another lesson from Africa.

Winnowing sorghum

In southern Uganda the staple food is steamed bananas. In the drier north, maize, millet and sorghum are worked into various dishes. Sorghum produces large plumes of seeds. These plumes are stored in those picturesque round bins where sun and wind keep them dry. Almost daily a needed portion of those plumes is taken out, thrashed, and winnowed in the wind, and ground into powder, which is then used for porridge or baked as patties.

Independence Day celebrations include a very naughty dance where the Ugandan flag forms the background for a strange performance that nobody wants to miss. Men dressed in leopard skins play the drums. Then six or seven women with protruding buttocks are picked to come up to the stage, and there to shake their buttocks provocatively in order to arouse the hundreds of specta-tors. After about ten minutes they stop this first warming-up part under loud applause, and take a well-earned gulp or two of banana beer. Seven other eager volunteers are then allowed up to the stage to try to bring the dance perhaps to a first climax. The purpose of their gyrations is to attract some impressive arousals out in the open. It's all done for fun. There's no harm in this game at all. The naughty dancers are watching the crowd to see what effects their rotating buttocks have, always hoping to witness a throbbing

Erection dance

erection. The swines! And yes, a few young men are eagerly collaborating by, in tune with the drumming, thrusting their hips and belly forward and backward.

And then it becomes a real celebration of life. A young man still a teenager probably, urges forward to the stage. Three dancers move back towards him, fluttering like birds of paradise in heat. With tens of women and teenage girls crowding around him the young man proudly produces a big triumphant erection under great applause. Life!

Bahima compound, Southern Uganda

This is the last major painting I did in Uganda, 1974. It is framed as a triptych.

I had a few Bahima students from this originally nomadic tribe of shepherds, and asked them for input. What is inside a hut? Where are things placed? How does your mother set up the evening meal? What do you do afterwards? My students were truly excited to give me authentic details. The blue uniforms of the girls indicate their elementary school. Boys must be naked during the meal and for the night. Chickens and goats are also inside the hut for the night for safety against marauding jackals.

Prepared for the dance

Dancing. I went to the Junior Seminary when I was 12 years old. The handbook of rules stated clearly that dancing may be all right as a preparation for marriage, but not for a seminarian. I never danced, but early on during a talent night at St. Mary's College I watched a group of students from one of the 16 tribes of Uganda perform a tribal dance. My spontaneous reaction was, "that's powerful. I never thought that dancing could be that beautiful!" I had been trained in my early years to distrust the natural impulses of the human body in search of physical contacts and harmonious movements. Another lesson learned in Africa.

The Karamojong were a small tribe in Uganda of some 100,000 people. But they fascinated me deeply because they were still so "primitively African", like their cousins the Turkana and Masai in Kenya.

I have based a disproportionate number of my paintings and sculptures on the lives of the Karamojong in the 1960's.

I had only one Karamojong student who turned out to be an exceptional artist. He told me that each time he came home from St Mary's College by bus he would, just before his village, take off all his clothes and greet his parents naked, as he should.

I learned from his artwork, as the next painting shows. The men of the village have just returned from a successful cattle raid, usually from another tribe, and each family is receiving one or two of the stolen cows. They are welcomed back home by the women.

Karamojong women welcoming cattle raiders back home

Only three tribes in eastern Uganda practise circumcision. The bachelor boys know that only circumcision will allow them to get married. When they are 17-18 years old they realize that they must face the music. In the presence of the village, and paying foreigners like me, they drop their trousers, spread their legs wide and present their genitals to a skilled elder. I noticed that the excitement had given all four candidates a convenient erection. With his left hand the elder grabbed the penis, and with the knife in his right hand he quickly slashed off two slices off the soft cock at the tip of the penis. The candidate managed not to winch. He rattled the iron chain over his shoulders and kept his arms defiantly above his head.

A few days later, when I was painting a landscape, the four newly circumcised boys, who had nothing else to do for the next six weeks except to heal, came around my easel and showed me how their penises were doing. They wore a soft towel around their waist with a stick firmly dug into their belly buttons to keep it away from their penises. From a distance they looked like heavily pregnant women.

Four bachelors presenting themselves for circumcision

The local tavern

Widows are encouraged by the village to turn their house into a tavern to ensure a livelihood. Other women are invited to turn their surplus of bananas or pineapples into beer and for a fee to the widow sell it to customers while sitting on a mat with her big gourd, and offer each customer a small sample of her personal brand. A recess in the back wall holds small drinking gourds dripping out after use. Overindulgence might lead to all sorts of minor mischief, the painting is suggesting.

Another Beer party

Wherever I saw people participating in a malwa, I knew that there was harmony in that area. Malwa is a pot of warm beer made from millet or sorghum with some sugar cane. People sit around it and suck the hot broth with a long reed, which in 1966 was a papyrus reed, but in 1974 a plastic one. It is easy to keep on sucking rather than letting it sink back into the pot. Therefore it can go to your head before you noticed it. In the background a man is starting to come down. The woman in the foreground, probably the owner of the place, is heating up more beer for a refill.

The men getting drunk on new banana beer

I made this painting in Kivu, an eastern province of the Congo. Missionaries there often came to Uganda for supplies that in 1967 were not available in the Congo. They invited me to come along with them for a holiday at their Mission, because they never had any visitors, they said, "and there are nice butterflies." I was amazed at the main three items that took most of the space in their panel truck: bags and bags of hosts, bags and bags of toilet paper, and several sets of car tires. Several missions and hospitals were counting on these purchases.

Every morning I would go out painting or sketching and the people were pleased that I had an interest in their villages. One morning I saw a scene of new banana beer being made. Mashed bananas and sugarcane had been stashed away three days ago into a hollowed-out tree trunk that had been partly dug underground to slow down the fermentation process. Now the time had come to taste the new brew. It must have been pretty good, because I saw a few men lolling half drunk on the ground. I made a sketch of it from a safe distance, and later worked it out into a detailed painting at the Rectory.

The missionaries were excited about my painting. One persuaded me to make a smaller version that would exactly fit in his suitcase, for he was soon retiring in Belgium.

But then his confrere used my painting during the Sunday service at the church to impress upon the people the evil of drunkenness. "Now our visiting priest is going to show in America what kind of drunk slobs you people are!" From that day on, I was never again so openly welcomed by them. To most Africans, drunkenness is not a disgrace or shame, but rather a forgiveable overindulgence for something that makes you feel good. One Sunday afternoon the two Belgian missionaries and I took a long walk to villages further away. We noticed one village where just about everybody was drunk or staggering about. The village chief came to invite us to visit his village, but we decided to demonstrably pass it by. In anger and desperation the chief threw up his hands and shouted *"Mais c'est notre nourriture!"*.

In traditional African society, the roles of men and women were clearly marked out. The men were the fighters and cattle raiders, protectors, and builders of the huts which lasted about seven years because of organic matter. Women were in charge of food production and the care of children. Their bodies were more solidly structured, and they were usually taller than men, because they do the daily chores at home and in the garden, while the men had lost their functions as fighters and protectors to the government.

A common tree around all the villages is the eucalyptus imported from Australia. It grows quicker than native African trees and is resistant to termites. Together with corrugated iron sheets for the roofs instead of grass, houses now remain standing for dozens of years. So, men had lost their functions when I arrived in Uganda in 1966. They often turned into slobs and drunkards. That created a big social problem for years to come.

Throughout 1973 storm clouds started to darken the sky in Uganda when Idi Amin's dictatorship broke out into mass murders, especially of two Nilotic tribes. The previous year he had already thrown out 60,000 Indians and Pakistanis who held a monopoly of Uganda's economy. Then as a "devout" Muslim he told all Israelis to leave. There were barely 100 of them, mostly training Uganda's fledgling air force personnel. When the Americans protested against these expulsions, they were ordered to leave. Untrained Africans took over the stores, and the economy ground to a halt. The new storekeepers happily sold out their inventory without calculating how and when to restock. In all this chaos it became evident that I could no longer safely hide behind my position of art teacher at leading Catholic college. I worked day and late evenings to record African life on canvas, knowing that I would be able to safely roll up paintings and return to the shelter of Canada, having a return ticket from CUSO in my pocket. Never did I go out at night to see a movie or go to a decent restaurant from mid-1973 on, because the army had control over the roads.

Idi Amin Out For a Snack

Leaving Uganda

Then the warning shot came from abroad where Amin's butcheries were much better known than in tightly controlled Uganda itself. My mother was developing ulcers while hearing the bad news from Africa. "If you want to see your mother alive," my sister wrote me," leave Uganda now." My chauffeur was getting nervous when I took my time collecting my suitcase and roll of paintings. In my ink drawing I selected the moment when the caterpillars of a large colourful moth are content to leave their food plant and start searching for a place to pupate and become something else. Some caterpillars are being squashed on the floor. It's all very symbolic.

Actually by Christmas 1973 I had completed more than the minimum contract with the Ugandan government for two complete schoolyears. So I left Uganda with all honour and allowance I was even given a military chauffeur to the airport.

But with a cruel parting shot of their unbridled Africanization, they kept the plane for over an unexplained hour on the tarmac. Only when we landed at our destination in Amsterdam, and our luggage was checked, did I and a few other ex-patriots notice that it had been pilfered from my meagre clothing my two best shirts were gone, and all money from the sale of insects mainly, was taken, even the Rand bills and British pounds that I had stuck all over my Breviary had been neatly removed. I should have known, for the army had stripped all expelled Asians, taken their jewelry and watches. Idi Amin and his soldiers found it easy to justify this large-scale robbery: "You Colonialists have milked the cow without feeding it."

However, my big treasure that I managed to take out of Africa was a fat roll of 60 paintings. Three of them I have on the wall right in front of me while I am writing these memories half a century later.

CHAPTER 4
RESETTLED IN CANADA?

Period of Nostalgia for Uganda in the 1970s.

Of course I couldn't avoid feeling a wistful yearning for the untrammeled freedom of selecting the inspirations I had experienced in Uganda.

In no time I had covered the walls of our spacious Community Residence with my African paintings. But then the Superior sidled up to me and said, "We appreciate your art, but we don't want to live in a museum." He assigned one major room for whatever I wanted to display, as well as the stairways and the basement. They have remained filled to the gills.

I am prolific.

Upon being urged by Idi Amin in 1974 to leave Uganda, I continued the same search for *'picturesque"* natural buildings in the Ottawa area. The one below, in Carlsbad Springs, was left untouched, with furniture and cupboards inside, because grandmother was still living in sight of her old home. However, a bunch of horses had a free run of the place and destroyed the weakened wooden floor.

Carlsbad Spring Farmhouse

CHAPTER 4: RESETTLED IN CANADA?

Within three days after my return to Canada I was appointed as art teacher & chaplain to Immaculata H.S., Ottawa, a girls' school with twelve and a half nuns on the staff, the half nun being the part-time librarian. I had hardly begun teaching my girls in early September 1974, when the Archbishop of Ottawa asked me if I was willing to take on the care of a small rural Irish parish as well. The 1970s were the peak period for priests to leave the priesthood and get married. It became more and more difficult for the bishops 'to man the parishes".

As result, on the weekends I drove for almost an hour to my small parish with a rectory attached to it. Halfway to my parish I would take gas at a station next to a railway line. Across from that one-track line was a rickety old farmhouse, practically a ruin, with horses around it, and the grounds strewn with rusty farm equipment.

"Whose property is that across the tracks?" I asked the owner of the gas station, while he was checking the oil.

"Mine," he said.

"Oh good," I said, " I would like to do a painting around it, if you don't mind."

"Oh you can't. We allow nobody to get onto the property, the horses and all that."

The next Saturday morning, as I was free from teaching on weekends, I returned to the CN track, plunked down my easel right on the track and started painting the glorious ruins. There was only one train that morning. It hooted from about a mile off till I removed my easel from the track.

Three hours later the gas station owner walked the track by stepping from tie to tie to see what I was up to. I knew he couldn't do anything against me because I worked on public property. He looked at my nearly finished painting and then at the treasure of his ruin for comparison.

"H'm, not bad. I'll send my two daughters to see it. Maybe they'll learn something. They take art in school."

A few months later I heard that the gas station owner was going to celebrate his 25th wedding anniversary. I gave this painting as a present to his oldest daughter. It hangs in the office of his garage, not in his home. What does that tell me?

My weekly trips to my parish gave me the benefit of seeing several simple landscape topics with trilliums growing under some old birches in early Spring just ahead of blackflies.

Triliums and Old Birches

It came as a revelation that I was glad to paint with almost no green. No wonder our "Group of Seven" avoided Summer and only started to paint landscapes earnestly in the Fall and then on till the snows disappeared in Spring; and that was not because of blackflies, etc. in the Summer (although I could see that this was a valid secondary excuse.)

In Uganda and Congo the steady tropical conditions had forced me to acclimatize myself to landscape painting with more and more deep green dominating the background.

And still, who can blame me for having my memory still in Uganda? Part of my brain was telling me to try and go back to Uganda when Field Marshal Idi Amin was driven out by rebels who were invading from Tanzania. I heard the anxious cry of my students, "You are not going to leave us now that things are getting tough, are you?" But it was becoming more and more unlikely that I would be able to return. Even Amin's successor turned out to be not much better, while I was getting tied down by work in the school and church.

So I sort of came to a compromise.

In Uganda I had concentrated on painting, for that was the only thing I had come to teach.

Now I poured all my energy in creating original African ceramic sculptures. I had a kiln available at school where I managed to teach as much sculpture as painting and graphics combined, and I had a kiln at home paid for by painting a set of Stations of the Cross for a priest-friend.

I am presenting here a set of the best ceramic sculptures I ever did. All of them were made in the years immediately following my leaving Uganda.

Let me start with one that's complex in structure, but easy to understand. One extended family huddle together to watch an unusual event: the arrival of a white man in the market.

Look Who's Entering the Market
(Ceramic, 1981)

"Look who's entering the market."

It expresses how I felt when as the only white man around would enter into an African activity. Everybody was watching you.

The next sculpture portrays a custom among Nilotic tribes, but not Bantu.

Among the Bantu tribes of Uganda the use of bark cloth for funerals is common. The dead person is wrapped in bark cloth sheets, and every participant in the burial contributes another sheet so that the bundle of wrappings becomes bigger, according to the number of friends and the wealth of that person. The actual burial takes place toward sunset on the day of the death, and it will take place in the family garden right between their banana trees. There is

Four Sons Carrying Father Wrapped in a Mat

more than a mere feeling that ancestors and departed relatives are near and somehow still involved in the welfare of the family.

I would spend maybe ten minutes at the beginning of the class discussing all these things before announcing, "And that will be your topic for the next three weeks or so, *a burial in my tribe.*"

"Shucks ", my only Karamojong Onek said. " Too bad, because in our tribe we don't have burials."

"Then what do you have?"

"The oldest sons will carry the corpse wrapped in a mat to a sacred tree, where the vultures will pick the bones clean."

"That's rather awkward to picture", I suggested.

"But what I will do is to present the actual funeral procession." he said.

So he did, but it never went beyond a rough sketch. Still, I found that sketch so vivid that I took it, and practically copied it in my own stiffer but clearer fashion. The woman in the foreground is in the process of constraining the grief-stricken woman bent in the dust before her.

Onek explained, "That woman is grieving ostentatiously because otherwise she might be accused of later sneaking up to the sacred tree and snatch parts of the body to eat."

A few tribes in the backwoods had indeed practiced cannibalism in the not too remote past.

Of course, a topic like *Karamoja Funeral* was highly attractive to me. The glazed ceramic sculpture I did of it is one of the finest art pieces I ever did....and one of the most difficult ones to make. Born with nothing, leaving with nothing. Africa has taught the West some valuable lessons about old age and dying. In African society the elderly are the most respected and honoured members of the extended family and neighbourhood. They are the ones with blood lines to many of the others, and they represent the experience and wisdom most others are lacking but hoping for. In tribal Africa, death does not really separate the departed ones from the living.

Karamojong Funeral

The Karamojong men of northern Uganda go entirely naked except perhaps for a goatskin cape fastened at the throat and loosely thrown over the shoulders in case it rains in that arid territory. We are reminded of the wise saying that in time of war, fathers bury their sons; in time of peace, sons bury their fathers. Especially when seen reduced to the bare minimum among these semi-nomadic herdsmen, such a funeral procession becomes a powerful symbol for the innate respect we humans must have for the passing generation, and at the same time it provides an instructive taste of our own aging and dying.

We, in North America are quite familiar with totem poles. The Haida still carve them today. These poles often embody the spirits of ancestors who are considered to still be around in these totem poles attached to the front of their homes.

African Motherhood Totem

Even more often, they incorporate the spirits of animals that threaten them like the bears, or who protect them like the clever raven who is seen as the creator of the human species by freeing them from oyster shells.

In my totem I replace spirits with living beings. Young children and nursing mothers are interwoven playfully to suggest the abstract idea of motherhood.

It goes without saying that biology determines a person's orientation. Naturally a woman's body is designed by evolutionary process to attract a man, to conceive and bear a child and breastfeed it. Noticeably in a tribal African society, the only fulfillment of womanhood is seen in the bearing and raising of children.

Without that, a woman is bound to feel incomplete and disoriented, as illustrated by the woman at the top of the totem (which is modelled after a Tanzanian batik design) Peer pressure can be mortally cruel.

It will take a great deal of intensive Christian teaching for such a *barren* woman to come to the acceptance of an alternative human completeness in dedication to community service, a sublimation that will require a gigantic effort and solid faith. This would best be done in connection with established church organizations and could take the form of care for widows, orphans, the elderly, or church ministries in music, sacristy work, Catechesis.

Another complex sculpture is the *Malwa*.

It was always an attractive sight to see a group of women sucking beer through long reeds (our plastic straws). After a while they would add hot water to the brew of millet or sorghum.

The backside of the sculpture with the bored kids is even more exciting to me. This particular glazed ceramic was purchased by the Ugandan High Commissioner at one of my public exhibitions. In the Nilotic tribes girls also, had to go through a period of initiation. The *Snake Dance* was an exercise in tribal togetherness.

Malwa

IT WAS ALWAYS AN ATTRACTIVE SIGHT TO SEE A GROUP OF WOMEN SUCKING BEER THROUGH LONG REEDS (OUR PLASTIC STRAWS). AFTER A WHILE THEY WOULD ADD HOT WATER TO THE BREW OF MILLET OR SORGHUM.

Via clay work and a plaster cast over a rubber mould. I had a Foundry cast a bronze with the usual allowance of six more casts. I made a second version in ceramic stoneware, which incorporated more anxiety and fear for the unknown.

By the end of 1979 I had thirty-nine, Ceramic African sculptures and I was ready for an exhibition. A few snatches of critique from the then two Ottawa newspapers will tell the story.

Snake Dance

Beauty Parlour
(Ceramic 18" h, 1980)

Thirty of the 39 sculptures were bought. As a matter of fact, presently I have only one of the original 39 left: a sculpture of three naked men chained together by their necks to be thrown to the crocodiles for daring to oppose the Kabaka, the former king of the Baganda tribe. It's so crude that nobody would want this on the mantelpiece. It will stay in a dark corner of my art studio till, after I am gone and somebody *accidentally* drops it.

At almost the same time as my Ufundi Gallery's exhibition, my first book, *From Uganda with Love* was published in New York. I have extensively described this in Chapter Two. Moreover, Archbishop M. Gervais, a classmate of mine from three years of Theology at St. Peter's Seminary in London, Ontario asked me if I could handle a larger parish in Ottawa, St. Monica's, for he was stuck. He asked me as a friend, for he knew my artwork and my full load of teaching. This constant involvement around Ottawa made me decide to put Uganda behind me for good. I had reached the point where I could say, I've done it all. Besides, in my mid-fifties I was coming to an age where life in disorganized, insecure Africa was losing its attractiveness.

CHAPTER 5
COPING WITH SERIOUS RELIGIOUS ART

Most art intends to celebrate the sacred and spiritual in life in such a way that the viewers become aware of the transcendent by way of sensory representations. The artwork in medieval churches dealt with God and the saints in heaven. A secondary theme was the punishments sinners were to receive in the afterlife where devils would torture them. Here the artists could finally find some room for light-heartedness and fun.

Those themes in church art were continued into our own age except that gradually all churches adopted a standardized set of 14 Stations of the Cross on the main interior walls of the building. The last quarter of the 20th century was a period of growth and prosperity for Canada. Millions of immigrants came to Canada and settled mostly in large cities, especially Toronto. The Archdiocese of Toronto saw itself obliged to build each year one new church. I was called upon to create new Stations of the Cross. I had a six-year contract with the Archdiocese from 1986-1992.

During my first year as pastor of St. Joan of Arc parish I observed a strange phenomenon: from September till May, the parish was a beehive of activities, and then towards the end of May all the meetings and committees came to an abrupt end. Nothing was going on except the Saturday weddings and Sunday services. This prompted me to make a set of Stations of the Cross each of the five remaining, summers annually to1992. It was not my natural choice of subjects, which lay more in the line of playfulness, but it was thrust upon me by existing needs and promptings by people in authority. And once I was involved in it. I made the best of it for the next several years. There is great sensual delight especially in the nude form, and in sculpture there is a feast for the eyes as well as for the sense of touch. It is a joy to celebrate life in the shapely human body, or in the playfulness between mother and daughter.

Mother and daughter
(Glazed stoneware, 1982)

The Prodigal Son

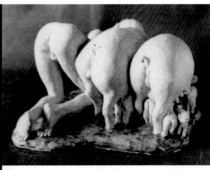

From the parable:
the prodigal son, feeding with the pigs

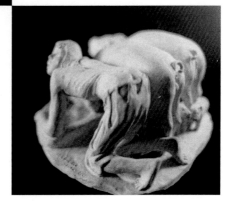

There is very little room in religious art for this kind of enjoyment of sensuality. However, I thought I had found it in the "Parable of the Prodigal Son', and I decided to use it. The writings of the New Testament show little evidence of humour or any form of levity.

"Repent. The end is near!" Christianity is basically an apocalyptic system of religion. Therefore, it is up to the artist to accentuate the humanness of some biblical stories, as I tried with my interpretation of this parable.

St. Luke's gospel describes the young man wasting all his money in reckless living. Then a severe famine spread over the land. So he went to work for one who sent him out to a farm to take care of his pigs. He wished he could fill himself with the bean pods the pigs ate.

I pictured him at the stage where he puts himself at the level of the pigs in order to get a share of the pigs' food. Naked he is like the other pigs, until remorse gets the better of him.

Ceramic Creche

Nativity sets allow for much freedom of expression. Ceramic is ideal for that. Real fun!

When around 1990 I was pastor of St. Joan of Arc in Toronto, Archbishop Ambrozic came for Confirmation. Just before the evening service I said to him, "if you want to change, use my room". When a few minutes later he returned in his purple regalia he said, "I saw your nice Nativity set. I would love to have it for my new residence".

Three weeks later I delivered this set, after I had added three kings, an ox and a donkey. I asked him which figurine he liked the most (expecting him to say, the boy on his stomach.) He said, "the sad donkey", thereby exposing his rural Croatian background.

When the nuns at Immaculata H.S. in Ottawa saw this ceramic sculpture, they smiled and said, "Nuns are no longer that way," and they put this very piece in their display case in the front lobby for all to see.

They shouldn't look at that!
(a Maillol Sculpture on a stand)

Girl With Dog Passing
("and they shouldn't look at that", the woman with the umbrella thinks)

Bent nude

THERE IS GREAT SENSUAL DELIGHT ESPECIALLY IN THE NUDE FORM, AND IN SCULPTURE THERE IS A FEAST FOR THE EYES AS WELL AS FOR THE SENSE OF TOUCH.

I GIVE THEM ALWAYS THE SAME POSITION OF THEIR ARMS, FOR THAT REALLY TELLS THEIR STORY. ADAM'S GESTURE SAYS, "HOW COULD I BE SO STUPID?"

The previous six sculptures all had some elements of humour. That might help you to now face the next twelve oh so serious, even dead-serious, sculptures.

I've done several Adam-and-Eve sculptures, each one slightly different. In this relatively recent version I omitted the belly buttons, because both were born without a mother. I give them always the same position of their arms, for that really tells their story. Adam's gesture says, "How could I be so stupid?"

But they still hold hands, for together they should be able to weather future storms.

The sculpture of Adam and Eve is the most appropriate one to lead on an anthology of biblical figures and scenes of the Passion of Christ.

Adam and Eve

———

Here is the well-known "Akedah", Abraham's binding of his only son Isaac. It is the struggle of Abraham with Jahweh about human sacrifices.

On the pedestal I portrayed a parallel human sacrifice of Jesus who also had to carry the wood of his own sacrifice, and is lamented by his own mother.

Three pages back I told the story of how Archbishop Ambrozic got his creche. A year later at the annual Confirmation Mass, I told him," If you want to change your vestments, use my room." A few minutes later he returned from my room carrying the sculpture of Abraham on his arm. "That's how I taught the Akedah in my bible classes. Can I buy it? How much?" Well, the year before I had freely given him the Nativity set, so I said, "Four hundred dollars." A few days later I got his cheque for $500. The next year I had him change his vestments in the sacristy.

The Akedah or Binding of Isaac

Moses

Similar in concept is the sculpture of Moses. I use the pedestal to portray four other episodes from the life of Moses: his being fished out of the Nile, the crossing of the Red Sea, the burning bush, and the descent from Mt. Sinai with the tablets of the Ten Commandments.

A sculpturally more dramatic event I kept for the top. At one time the travelling 12 tribes had to fight a heavy struggle against a confederation of local desert tribes. As long as Moses was able to keep his arms raised in prayer to Yahweh, the Jewish tribes prevailed.

Samson

The story of Samson has been acted out in several operas. Again I used the pedestal to portray four other episodes of life such as the two shown here: his managing to subdue a young lion, and his thoughtless submission to Delilah, who eagerly cuts off his hair, the magic source of his strength. For the top I kept a sculpturally more dramatic event. With his eyes gauged out and his body clown-like painted for mockery, Samson regains his super human strength to destroy himself with the temple of the Philistines.

After my "Prodigal Son", this became for the 1990's my most popular sculpture. It appeared on the cover of *Living with Christ*, a monthly missal for many churches. I managed to fulfil requests that came from California, Ottawa, Nova Scotia, and Rome Italy. The original (and my best) went by mail to California.

Lazarus (Ceramic on onyx, 17" h., 1990)

The parish I was pastor of from 1986 to 1992 was in the heart of Toronto on Bloor St., right across from a subway station. It had a parking lot and a spacious hall wonderful for art exhibitions, I thought. So, from 1988 on I organized an annual exhibition of spiritual art around a given theme. From my own sales of art I issued a art prizes and even bronze medals of honour with St. Joan of Arc on it, the name of the parish with the year, and, "Art Credo" the name I gave to the show. As I was the treasurer of the Sculptors Society of Canada, I had always at least a dozen fellow sculptors participating, Jews, Christians and Buddhists alike. Each participant had to submit one artwork on the given theme, and could then also bring one or two other works.

The themes ranged from "Strong Women in the Bible", "The Life of Christ from Birth to Death" to "Parables". This last one was most popular and produced many Good Samaritans and Prodigal Sons.

Good Samaritan Loading Donkey (Ceramic, 1989)

Surprisingly, three of the seven versions of the Prodigal Son were "Prodigal Daughters."

When after my agreed term of six years I left for a smaller parish in Ottawa (I was 64 by then) my successor who was less interested in art than in the perfect appearance of walls, sent me an angry note on a dozen nail holes that were left after the last "Art Credo" exhibition.

I FOUND A FINE BLOCK OF WHITE PINE THAT SENSUOUSLY FOLLOWS THE CONTOURS OF HIS BARE BACK, AND CONTRASTS WELL WITH LOWER VEGETATION.

Book of Job

The man Job, sitting outside on some old straw just as we do in connection with the corona virus, Job is asking himself the natural question if God has anything to do with human suffering even when he has led a God-fearing life. After 50 chapters, the biblical *Book of Job* still cannot reach a satisfactory answer, except to assert that "I know that my Redeemer lives." I made a great number of crucifixes through the years, this one using coat hanger wiring with papier mâché.

Crucifixion

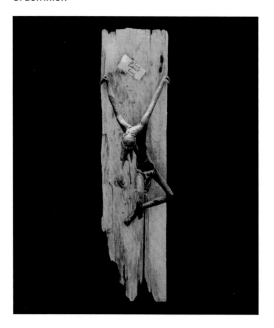

I never made comfortable, conventional ones. My crucifixes are meant to make you cringe and look away in embarrassed silence.

At one time after Mass, a parishioner stopped me and said, "Father, our daughter is getting married and we would like to give her one of your crucifixes for their new home." Then her smile turned into a thoughtful reflection, and she added. "But not one of your painful ones. Couldn't you make us one where Jesus is smiling?"

Station 4 – Condemnation

I have made twelve sets of Stations of the Cross, seven for the Toronto region, four for Ottawa, and one for Mississippi, U.S.A. Just imagine the thousands of hours that most have taken. Each set of 14 stations has its own history, but the set for the U.S.A. had a peculiar history. A town between Baltimore and Washington had converted its church with 1000 seats. In *Chit Chat* magazine for wood carvers they had read an article about my wood carving and seen an illustration of one my Stations of the Cross I got a letter from the parish council that they had decided that they wanted stations carved by me. I answered that I was hesitating because I had guidelines from the Vatican. The stations should be broader than just the *Via Dolorosa* from Pilate to burial. They should be scriptural, and therefore leave out legendary elements like Veronica, the three falls, and Mary meeting Jesus on the way to Calvary. The Vatican guidelines also demanded five new stations namely the Last Supper the Agony in the Garden, the Judgement of the Sanhedrin, the Flogging and Crowning with Thorns, and Jesus' Resurrection.

Station 5 – The Scourging

I wrote back to that American Parish Council that it would be wise to first see more of my set because it was rather revolutionary, and that I would drive down to them with half of my set to see.

They were happy with my cautious approach. I drove down with seven of my set: three traditional ones, and four "revolutionary" ones, like the scourging with the suggestion of the crowning with thorns.

The next morning I brought the seven stations to the big new church where carpenters and electricians were still buzzing around for the last touches. Three prominent council members with an elderly Irish pastor were present when I put the pieces on display on the seats of the first pew. The four of them were humming and hawing while shifting from one station to another. "Is that the first station, The Last Supper?"

"You see Father", said the pastor to me in an aside, "my parishioners are quite traditional." And I thought, you almost in the outskirts of Washington have more lawyers and doctors than most other places.

Even "The Agony in the Garden", my favourite station, was only partially understood with the trance-like anticipation of the Crucifixion in the background.

The four of them were at an impasse till I suggested that I could leave them there so that all the parishioners would be able to see them.

"So we can send them back to you if they are not accepted by the rest?"

"Yes, under one condition: that you pay me for my expenses by the price of one station.

Two weeks later I had them back in Ottawa, with a check for $500.

Ironically the set ended up in Mississippi, near Memphis, Tenn. But the pastor there had them framed, I heard. Unnecessary!

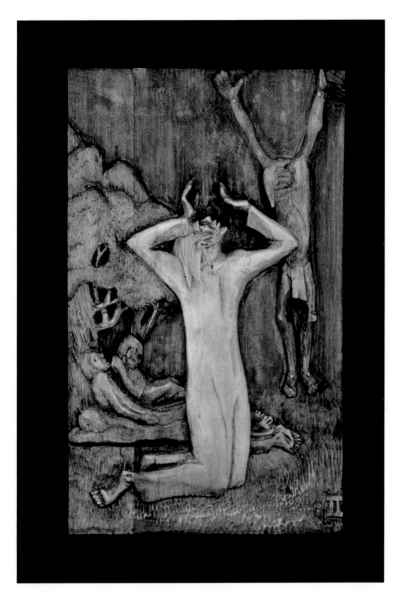

Station 2
The Agony in the Garden

Station 11
Between Mary and John

This eleventh station is now officially called "Mary and John". It is actually the first station where genuine human emotions can be portrayed. I used that opportunity greedily. And effectively, I hope...

For about 20 years, I was mainly occupied with creating complete sets of 14 stations. But on the side I made other individual pieces of religious art of the Passion for private persons. It gave me an opportunity to focus on seemingly unimportant details, such as throwing dice to decide who was going to get the above-average tunic of Jesus.

Rolling Dice for Clothing

Ecce Homo

Another such extraordinary detail of the Passion is the "Ecce Homo" when Pontius Pilate hopes that a display of a naked, fully scourged Jesus, might give Jesus a last chance to escape crucifixion. It had more the opposite effect.

The "Ecce Homo" scene was not selected as one of the new stations, possibly in order not to give too much exposure to Pontius Pilate.

And It Grew Dark

Humiliation was intended and the victims were usually naked: they had lost all rights to dignity and privacy. Still we can understood why most Christians find it uncomfortable to look at a naked Christ crucified. "He became like us in everything except sin." But we prefer to create an artificial exception here. My crucifixes are intended to make people uncomfortable for a moment of personal reflection on how unconditional Jesus' love for us was.

"At noon the whole country was covered with darkness, which lasted for three hours."
Matthew 27:45

Landscape painting became more and more occasioned as I was getting older and more occupied indoors. But after that heavy anthology on religious topics I needed a break before we go into woodcarving.

The painting of "Village Perce" I made on a camping trip with my oldest brother and his wife. I spent most of two days on it. When I was finished, I said, "And now I am going for a swim."

"You are?" a sunbather said, getting on his elbows to watch this. "Yes I am", I said, "I've earned it." I dashed into the North Atlantic, but did not even go in as far as my knees. The water was ice cold, not more than 6° Celsius.

Village Percé, Easternmost Quebec

Lanark Swamp (Two very typical landscapes near Ottawa)

Farrelton on the Gatineau River

A priest-friend of mine who had moved to Arizona because of a bronchial condition asked me to take his place in a Phoenix parish for the month of August while he went on a trip to Rome and the Holy Land. Since I had my summer holidays from teaching. I accepted the invitation. Practically every day the temperature went well over 100°F, but everything was air-conditioned, soon I discovered how beautiful the Sonora Desert was for painting. So on each of my weekly free days I would wake up by alarm clock at five, be in the desert at six, and paint till noon with a gallon of water at my feet, and sleep it off in the afternoon. At the end of August I showed off my six desert paintings at a choir rehearsal. "That's cool", one of the singers said. "Our artists here only paint in the desert after the rains in Spring, when everything is in bloom."

Sonora Desert

Still, at the end of this mainly dark chapter, part of me says I should apologize for the sadness I portrayed in the Passion of Christ. Is that a celebration of life?

Or is it my indulgence into sensationalism?

In facing the horrible injustice imposed by narrow-minded politicians and religious leaders on Jesus Christ, we must look to our faith in a loving God.

The history of the Judeo-Christian religion from the first thinking people who expressed awareness of an attentive Supreme Being to the great Jewish prophets shows that this Yahweh is actually madly in love with us. "Madly" is the keyword here. The charismatic Jew, Jesus Christ became the personification of that divine madness.

"God is love" is not an empty phrase.

It is a reality, and at the same time a mystery for us myopic mortals.

As St. Paul writes, "What we see now is like the dim image in a mirror; then we shall see face to face. What I know now, is only partial; then it will be complete" (I Cor 13:12)

So yes, the Passion of Christ is still a celebration. But one without balloons and confetti.

CHAPTER 6
MY DRAMATIC SHIFT TO WOODCARVING

Having worked with clay nearly all my life, ceramic sculpture became second nature to me. Yet something was missing, or rather two things. I wished I could work in a medium that was stronger and more enduring than baked clay, and that allowed me to do larger sculptures. My kiln was only 14" wide and 16" high inside. I thought I had been clever in producing larger ceramic sculptures by doing them in parts that fit together, glued with epoxy on top of each other, as I showed in Chapter 5 with the sculptures of Abraham, Moses, and Samson.

Anyway, I took a course in stone carving and spent a whole summer carving away lustily with power tools on local limestone and brucite. Clouds of dust swirled around in our small backyard. One talkative neighbour leaned on our fence and wondered what harm could come from all that dust. I tried to convince him that limestone dust was good for his lawn. Another neighbor complained about the dust on his windowsills. And then to top it all, a confrere stepped outside and snapped, "Can't you make any other noise?"

Fortunately for all the victims of my stone carving I was transferred to Toronto as pastor of St. Joan of Arc parish on Bloor Street.

After a while I discovered that at the Etobicoke Academy of Art there was a good course in woodcarving taught by Ruth Badzo, For a whole year from 1991 to 1992, I attended her weekly three-hours course, and it changed the direction of my art.

Ruth Badzo's teaching method fit me to a T. The students first had to work out their chosen topic in clay, and from that moist clay-model sketch it on the basswood board. Many of the students struggled for two or three weeks with the clay model, while I took it home, finished and dried it, and fired it in my kiln just in time for the second carving lesson. I even had it already sketched out on my basswood board, ready for carving. Ruth looked at it wide-eyed, and gave her smiling approval My key to success was that I turned my weekly three hours at school into 20 hours of progress at home, while all the other students took their work home for safety and then brought it back to class a week later, untouched. Ruth taught some useful lessons on how to use the various chisels and how to keep them sharp.

After the first month I had finished my piece, and Ruth called the whole class of 24 together to hear her critique of that first piece finished that year in her class. By Christmas, I finished three

After marble reliefs of Ivan Mestrovic
(Butternut, 20"x8", 1999)

pieces while all the others were still struggling with their first one, at the end of the school year there was the National Canadian Exhibition of Woodcarving, held that year in Toronto, and Ruth was one of the judges. She said that it was the first time ever that a student of hers was invited to participate, but she persuaded me to submit ten of my modest pieces next to well-known carvers from all over Canada. Still, I managed to receive three second and third-place money prizes for three of my carvings.

And I made my first sale of a woodcarving to an elderly lady in our class who had been watching the speedy progress I made on four wild horses while she was struggling for more than half a year on her unicorn. I had arrived!

Some sculptures present a sheer delight to the touch by their forms. The French artists Maillol and Despiau are famous for that.

However, several kinds of wood add an attractive grain and inner design to that delight.

The lute player, modelled after a marble sculpture by Mestrovic from Croatia, illustrates this well by the contrast of the smooth exaggerated female shape with the rough background. This illustration introduces me to point out some advantages that wood has over other media. I will illustrate each of these advantages with one of my own works.

Here are these advantages as I see them.

1. Wood can come in bulky blocks that can easily be shaped with a saw.
2. Many even local species of wood like butternut and ash, have attractive surfaces.
3. Wood easily allows freedom of shape.
4. Irregular tree cuts can lead to playful improvisations.
5. Bark left on can provide a natural framing.
6. Wood panels allow large compositions.
7. Wood naturally grows upward and thus becomes suitable for tall sculptures.
8. Sometimes a repeated pattern in the wood can be used to advantage for a special topic.
9. Low relief carving could reduce the required thickness of the panel to within an inch, thus reducing the weight of large panels.
10. In wooded areas of Canada, wood is readily available and inexpensive.
11. It is easy to repair wood when it breaks. And if a wood carving simply failed, or frustrates you with unexpected knots or cracks, you can turn it into firewood.

Mary and Elizabeth
(Butternut, 20"x12"x4", 1997)

1.
SOMETIMES WOOD IS AVAILABLE IN LARGER CHUNKS

Mary visiting her cousin Elizabeth who is pregnant with John the Baptist.

I get most of my wood in boards one to two inches thick. But occasionally I see an attractive block for an all-round sculpture, like this butternut sculpture of the Visitation. Sometimes people bring me chunks of trees that have come down in their backyard. Sometimes they prove to be useful; at other times... firewood!

Peekaboo
(Butternut, 20"x11"x14", 2001)

Baby feeling safe between its mother's legs.

The biblical story from early Genesis, about Abraham's cousin Lot and his wife and two daughters. Only those four are allowed to escape from the doomed town of Sodom, provided they do not look back. Poor wife of Lot! Salt.

2.
SOME WOODS HAVE ATTRACTIVE SURFACES.

I have a preference for butternut, precisely because it produces wonderful patterns, less ostentatious than oak (which is fine for furniture.)

Crossing the Red Sea
(White pine, 24"x14", 2000)

Ballerina Suzanne Farrell

3.
WOOD PROVIDES A SURPRISING FREEDOM OF SHAPE.

You must watch the structure of the wood, especially if you have legs sticking out loosely as the sulking angels have. Otherwise... have your glue ready. Whenever I had siblings visiting me from Holland, I let them chose one of my sculptures. My sister selected this ballerina pair; my brother Ben took the Mestrovic lute player
(found back on page 93)

Raphael's sulking angels, in third dimension
(White pine, 15"x12", 1997)

Large oval of the Nativity
(White pine, 51"x24", 2005)

**4.
YOU MUST GO TO LOCAL PRIVATE
SAWMILLS TO PICK IRREGULARLY
SHAPED BOARDS ON WHICH YOU CAN
IMPROVISE LIKE NOBODY ELSE.**

Even a discarded slice of a branch brought me to the idea of the young David hiding with three friends in a crack of a mountain when his archrival King Saul squats in front of them to relieve himself.

David and Saul at a grotto (Black walnut, 39"x8", 2006)

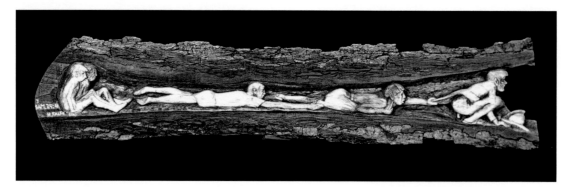

Hollywood Fare
(Basswood, 44"x16", 2004)

"Hollywood Fare" hung for several years above our T.V. till a family from my last parish bought it off our wall. The "Fare" of adventure, glamour, and entertainment are represented by Clint Eastwood, Marilyn Monroe, and Charlie Chaplin. Swirling cellophane links them together.

5.
AGAIN, AT LOCAL SAWMILLS YOU CAN EASILY AND CHEAPLY SELECT BOARDS THAT STILL HAVE THE BARK ON BOTH SIDES TO PROVIDE NATURAL FRAMING. THAT INDICATES THAT THE WOOD WAS PROCESSED IN LATE FALL OR WINTER WHEN THE BARK IS FIRMLY CONNECTED TO THE WOOD OF THE TREE.

Studio with sculptures alive
(White pine, 39"x24", 1998)

6.
WOOD FACILITATES LARGER COMPOSITIONS THROUGH LAMINATION. FOR MY STATIONS OF THE CROSS I HAD THE "WOOD SOURCE" YARD IN MANOTICK, ON LAMINATE A SET OF 14 BOARDS OF KNOT-FREE WHITE PINE 24"X18" OR LARGER.

"Life in my studio" is my favourite sculpture. I'm happy that good friends bought it. All the various types of sculpture I produced are represented, although religious works dominate. The sculpture I am working on blesses my endeavours.

Noah's Ark
(Cedar, 59"x12", 2005)

This sculpture of Noah's Ark, and "earth mother" in the next chapter illustrate this well.

In using wood in its natural shapes before the commercial world automate their machines to turn it into 2x4's and standard boards, I have stumbled upon a unique form of sculptural expression.

I am really celebrating that!

An answer provided to the question, "how did Noah get all those animals, even in pairs, into the arc?" The answer lies in a skyscraper approach.

7.
BECAUSE TREES GROW-UPWARD, TALL SCULPTURES ARE EASILY PRODUCED. I HAVE MADE GOOD USE OF THIS ADVANTAGE THAT IS UNIQUE TO WOOD.

The Olympics always produce a series of fine action poses. The Czechoslovakian stamp of 1980 is highly imaginative.

1980 Czechoslovakian Olympic stamp
(White ash, 23"x15", 1997)

The Olympic postage stamp shows off the attractive grain in white ash to its advantage.

8.
CERTAIN SPECIES OF TREES PROVIDE ATTRACTIVE SURFACES, AND OTHERS DON'T. FOR INSTANCE BASSWOOD IS EXCELLENT FOR QUICK AND EASY CARVING, BUT HAS A DULL, UNATTRACTIVE SURFACE, ALMOST INVITING YOU TO COVER IT WITH PAINT. IN ORDER OF PERSONAL PREFERENCE I HAVE FOUND THE FOLLOWING LOCAL SPECIES WORTH-WHILE FOR THEIR PLEASANT WOODGRAIN: BUTTERNUT, WHITE ASH, WHITE PINE, AND EASTERN CEDAR.

White pine, 48"x23", 1997

This large sculpture was created in a transitional time when Catholics still felt duty-bound to go to church on Sundays. But what many did there, had little to do with religion, down to Sudoku and sleeping. The clergy was getting very old and boring.

Details of priest

I used a typically ancient confrere for the priest, and five of my own Stations of the Cross in the background.

I had this, "Congregation taxed to the limit" at an exhibition in Milwaukee, Wisconsin. The superior of a major Seminary nearby bought it for $1.200. Apparently he wanted to use it to impress upon his seminarians how not to preach.

9.
YOU CAN MAKE WOODCARVINGS AS LIGHT-WEIGHT AS YOU WANT. I HAVE PRODUCED BAGS OF WOODCHIPS, TO START FIRES, BY HOLLOWING OUT THE BACK OF LARGE SCULPTURES TILL I'D BREAK THROUGH TO THE SURFACE.

One day I was driving up a country road to our summer cottage near the Gatineau River. A deer with three points' antlers stood in the road. I stopped the car, and we looked at each other for maybe three seconds till the deer graciously jumped the fence into a neglected pasture. I stepped out to see if I could still spot it further up. That's when I discovered the saw mill with only some end pieces lying around. I found the house of the owner nearby and asked him if I could get one or two end pieces. I then presented him one of my art books to show how I used naturally shaped pieces of wood for my carving. He smiled and then said: "I have better wood for you. Come with me." We climbed a ladder to the top floor of his barn and there was a stack of 12 feet long boards of white pine, one inch thick and separated neatly by small slats of wood for the wind to dry them. Twenty-three inches wide, all of them.

Mother and child (White pine, 40"x23", 1996)

10.
WOOD FOR THE CONSTRUCTION OF HOUSES AND FLOORS IS ONE OF CANADA'S LARGEST EXPORTS. WOOD IS ABUNDANTLY AVAILABLE ALL OVER CANADA. A FRIEND OF MINE MADE HIMSELF A MILLIONAIRE BY GATHERING HARDWOOD LIKE MAPLE AND OAK IN THE OTTAWA VALLEY AND CUT IT UP FOR PARQUET FLOORS FOR EXPORT TO JAPAN AND DRY COUNTRIES IN NORTH AFRICA. IN THE PROCESS OF COLLECTING HARDWOOD AT SAWMILLS, HE ALSO COLLECTED BUTTERNUT FOR ME. HE BOUGHT SEVERAL OF MY WORKS INCLUDING THE VERONICA FOUND IN CHAPTER THREE.

I was mouthwatering when he said to me: "I'll let you have one if you make a Madonna sculpture, for the wife, *pour la femme*, who wants me to make a gazebo from these boards."

I asked him how he got the wood. He explained that he was no longer a real farmer. He used his land for some beef cattle and some hay for the winter. He worked for Ontario Hydro and spent his days keeping the wires free. One day when he was doing that job, a lady comes up to him and said:" I have a mature big white pine growing next to my house. I'm afraid that one day a big branch will break off and damage the house. Could you cut it down for me? I will pay you for it."

The next free day, Saturday, he got the needed equipment, and brought the lower trunk of 12 feet to his own sawmill. In that way he got his magnificent knot-free white pine boards, and got paid for it as well. Opportunity knocks.

He cut my board into three pieces of 48" each, so that I could transport them in my care. One piece I turned into the "Congregation taxed to the limit", the previous sculpture, and the second into this sticky rainy summer day with mother and baby boy leaning against the window, and the third... I forgot where that went. Or what it became.

11.
I HAVE AN ELEVENTH ADVANTAGE THAT WOOD HAS OVER SEVERAL OTHER MEDIA, AND THAT IS THAT A BREAK IN WOOD CAN BE REPAIRED EASILY, BECAUSE SUCH BREAKS ARE ALWAYS CLEAN. CARPENTER'S GLUE WILL DO THE JOB. I HESITATED ABOUT MENTIONING THIS ADVANTAGE, BECAUSE IT IS SO DIFFICULT TO ILLUSTRATE. I KEEP MY REPAIRS AS INVISIBLE AS POSSIBLE, AND I'VE LEARNED HOW TO SUCCEED IN THAT.

Fountain Sculpture

However, recently I pulled from my junk heap an old grey chunk of wood that had the shape I needed for a specific purpose. In an article on Brasilia, Brazil I had seen an attractive bronze sculpture in a fountain in front of the new Imperial Palace. I asked a friend who works in External Affairs and travels much, to take a photo of that sculpture for me. He tried but was resolutely refused to come near it. So near the palace, *No Admittance* means *No Admittance*. However, he found a postcard.

My miserable piece of wood proved to be as uncooperative as I have experienced in no other chunk of wood. Both heads broke off and all four arms broke in at least one place. Then both torsos broke in the middle section. Glue, glue. Normally I would avoid spending my time and energy on a flawed chunk of wood. But that month of July, 2020 had a long hot spell that allowed me any excuse to spend long hours in my basement studio where the temperature was nearly 10 degrees cooler The final product looked as if it had gone through Hurricane Hazel. So I turned to my last resort: paint. The final result looks like a strange compromise between marble and bronze; Still better than another piece of firewood.

Jonah riding the waves
before being beached

Finally I want to round off this chapter on wood carving with eight of my most entertaining pieces of sculpture that otherwise may fall between the cracks. It would be a pity if you missed them

The biblical, fictional character of Jonah is so human and so flawed that he becomes likeable, like the German prankster Till Eulenspiegel. A sea monster swallows him up, the story goes, and carries him to Nineveh where he had refused to go.

Anyway the main point of this late book of the Old Testament is that God should not be seen as a national Jewish God, but rather as one who has mercy and love for the whole human race. An appropriate message for modern times, too.

Jonah inside the whale

Two men went up the temple to pray
(White pine, 38"x36", 2007)

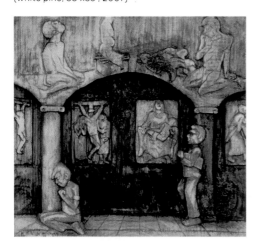

I gave this biblical story a Catholic setting, for also in our time there are people going to church telling God, "You must be happy to see me, because I am so pious, so good, and not a scoundrel like that guy there..."

The Parable of the Pharisee and the Tax Collector

Jesus also told this parable to people who were sure of their own goodness and despised everybody else. "Two men went up to the temple to pray; one was a Pharisee, the other a tax collector. The Pharisee stood apart by himself and prayed, 'I thank you, God that I am not greedy, dishonest, or immoral, like everybody else; I thank you that I am not like that tax collector. I fast two days every week, and I give you one tenth of all my income. But the tax collector stood at a distance and would not even raise his face to heaven, but beat on his breast and said, 'God, have pity on me, a sinner!' I tell you," said Jesus, "this man, and not the other, was in the right with God when he went home. Because everyone who makes himself great will he humbled, and everyone who humbles himself will be made great.

Luke, 18-9

The low-relief scene above the arches refers to the Old Testament event of the sacrifices brought by Cain and Abel. The prayer of the humble tax collector rises up just like the sacrifice of Abel, while the prayer of the Smug Pharisee just like Cain's sacrifice, is rejected by God.

Paul Tex Lecor, Choir rehearsal (1981)

Every parish has some sort of a choir where people sing, some good, some average, and others... well..., but always with great dedication to the praise of God and the devotional needs of the parishioners.

Line-ups for the telephones, what's that? For the new generation it's a vague memory of the past.

Telephone cells occupied (White pine, 44"x20", 2000)

A complicated, large sculpture, "vernissage to an exhibition of my own sculptures." I had two purposes for this work.

First I wanted to retain some visible evidence of the six sculptures that I had recently sold: the loving couple, Raphael's sulking angels, the Prodigal Son, the creation of Eve from Adam's ribs, the Annunciation, and Karamojong funeral.

Second I tried to create a *"trompe l'oeille"* in that the background recedes endlessly. I did that by having this complete sculpture hanging as a sculpture on the back wall partly behind the waitress and some guests. You try that trickery only once.

Vernissage (White pine, 42"x23", 2000)

The New Testament

A servant girl asked Peter in the courtyard of the High Priest, "Aren't you one of the disciples?" Peter shrugged his shoulders and said, "Jesus of Nazareth? Never heard of him". But the rooster was about to crow.

Almost immediately after his denial of Jesus, Peter repented, and felt terribly small.

Repentant Peter

Last Supper
(White pine, 53"x31", 1997)

The house of my Religious Community in Ottawa used to be the Japanese Embassy until Pearl Harbor, December 1941. We converted the wood-paneled reception hall into our chapel. I found the space above the fireplace and mantelpiece an ideal place for a sculpture of the Last Supper, 53"x 31". However, I composed the well-known scene of Christ breaking bread and sharing the cup with his twelve apostles in an abstract way in order to convey the spiritual meaning of this most fundamental act of the Christian liturgy: through our participation in the Eucharistic meal we become one spiritual community.

To the young generation I add one more piece of information: only Christ has 20-20 vision.

CHAPTER 6: MY DRAMATIC SHIFT TO WOODCARVING

As early as the year 1387, a certain Geoffrey Chaucer wrote a sizeable work of prose and poetry that could be considered the real start of English literature. And surprisingly it is an entertaining piece of writing because, in contrast to the usual fare of the time that dealt with mythological figures and imaginary heroes, Chaucer dealt with common people involved in common activities. The story line is simple: 24 pilgrims travel together from London to the shrine of Saint Thomas Becket in Canterbury. A host and a bagpiper lead a motley group of local officials and merchants, monks, a prioress with her white hound dogs, and other pious commoners on towards Canterbury. To break the monotony of the many hours in the saddle the host proposes that for the prize of a fine meal in Canterbury, each pilgrim should tell one story. These tales with the commentaries that follow them, make up Chaucer's book, "The Canterbury Tales". Some stories, like the Wife of Bath, are bawdy, while others like the one of the parish priest are edifying.

I hesitated including this piece, because I closely followed an old engraving... but then you would have missed a charming piece of work.

Canterbury pilgrims

CHAPTER 7
MY ART REFLECTING CRISES OF THE TIME

Idi Amin's cruel dictatorship and attempts to genocide had forced me to leave Uganda in 1974. In a way we were fortunate that he did not dare to harm foreigners like the Asiatics, British or North Americans, and restrict himself to merely robbing them, as my ink drawing pictures taking place on an isolated road through a national park, with only baboons and dung beetles as witnesses. Don't look too deeply for symbolism. At least we could get out alive.

That was the second dictatorship I survived, after Hitler and his Nazis, that is.

Leaving Africa, I accepted an invitation of the same Fréres de l'Instruction Chrétien, F.I.C.'s that I had lived with in Uganda, to visit them soon at their international school in Japan. I was offered the same combination of art teaching and chaplaining. I spent part of my leisure time picking out and describing ten lovely spots for painting in the future, especially around some old temples in Kyoto. Almost 50' years later those spots are still unpainted. I started to appreciate the charm of Japanese culture and its moderated forms of Buddhism.

One day I stood in front of a Catholic Church, and I stopped to apologize in my heart to Japan for that church. It looked as if it was there transferred from a small Italian town. I felt sorry for what my arrogant Catholic Church was trying to muddle up here. But then I had seen the same sort of imposition of R.C. culture in primitive Karamoja, Uganda. I had gone there with two teaching Brothers to experience the peculiar attractiveness of that remote region. We entered the church, and looked around silently, till one of us said, "Where are we? In Apulia or Calabria?" Let's sit down and see if we can find anything that is not Italian." We did. Wooden pews, a communion railing, a statue of St. Anthony, and to add insult upon injury, stations of the cross with Italian texts on them (probably for the benefit of

Amin's soldiers on a rampage

the nuns attached to school and church.) Finally one of us discovered one item you wouldn't find in Apulia: an electric sanctuary light instead of one using olive oil.

Well, the Catholic Church has been successful in absorbing most of the ancient cultures in Europe, the Americas, and is well on its way to do the same in Sub-Saharan Africa.

But in Japan? No way! I'm praying against them.

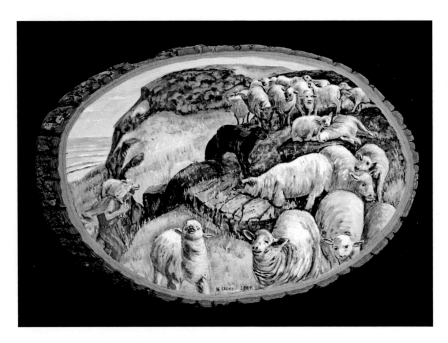

The Prodigal Son

The Pre-Raphaelite painter W.H. Hunt painted in 1852 a work called "Our English Coasts (Strayed Sheep)". These "strayed sheep" were intended to illustrate the inadequacy of volunteer soldiers against a potential French invasion of England. It became, of course, easy in later years to give the painting a Christian connotation. I blatantly obliged by introducing at the lower left a shepherd who brings up from the steep ravine a lost sheep.

Returning to Canada in 1974, I landed into a changing world. The new generation of Catholics no longer accepted unquestioningly Vatican indoctrination. Clergy was leaving in droves; nuns and religious societies like the one I belong to were no longer able to attract new candidates.

Pressure was put upon me to accept more and more parish work, although I had never really been trained for that. Fortunately I had the ability to delegate many functions in the parish to eager and capable lay people, like maintenance, finances, baptism and marriage preparation.

In this way I always managed to keep enough time free for my art work. I never was a "Good Shepherd" in the traditional sense of unre-served commitment.

I never felt guilty about that, because I was trained and commissioned to teach in secondary schools.

Our Brazilian Superior Writes

———

"This sculpture is lasting reminder of our link and boundaries, of our belonging to one another and our friendship. During the year of our jubilee, 2008, the sculpture will wander in our Province from community to commu-nity, showing the goodness of a divine heart open to everyone who comes across his way." The Good Shepherd, blessed by Pope John Paul II before it travelled through Brazil in 2002.

Just because the entrenched, unbudging Church was holding back on modern progress, including equal rights for women and democracy, and therefore was losing its clergy, was not reason enough for me to abandon art and teaching, and wholeheartedly jump on the bandwagon of the Church with its tires going flat. Helping out to keep a sinking ship afloat became more and more fighting for a lost cause.

I maintained my small portion of that for the sake of so many sincere faithful of the older generations. But I was not qualified to stand up and challenge the establishment on a higher level to bring about radical changes that impact the deeper theological and psychological impasse of the Church. I tried it once, in 1996. There was a group of progressive "Catholics of Vision" who expressed their objection to efforts of the higher hierarchy to propose that priests cannot follow their conscience and promote discussion of issues like the need for lay input into Catholic sexual teachings and a reversal of the ban on communion for divorced and remarried Catholics, and a greater role for women in Church affairs.

One Sunday in a written-out, well-prepared sermon I stated that I supported the progressive stand of the "Catholics of Vision", and that I was even "open to accept women as priests, like the Anglican pastor we have here in Osgoode. Therefore, I must disagree with Cardinal Ratzinger (the future Pope Benedict XVI) who has written that we are not even permitted to discuss the possibility of allowing women to be ordained to the priesthood, because Jesus only chose men as his priests. If Ratzinger's argument holds true, then only circumcised Galileans can be ordained to the priesthood."

I added that I wasn't proposing women's ordination immediately everywhere, because some countries like India or the USA might not be ready for that now. But I felt Ratzinger was wrong in trying to decide for all ages to come what should not be allowed.

Rules and human regulations change through the ages, and they will, and should, for the future. Making categorical decisions about human regulations is like locking them up in a drawer and then throwing away the key.

I invited my parishioners to pick up some literature I had about the "Catholics of Vision". Seven parishioners dropped off envelopes with money to support this movement. But then hell broke loose.

Citizen Tue. 4 Feb '97

Priest ordered to stop urging reform

Bishop forbids priest to endorse female, married priests

By Bob Harvey
Citizen religion and ethics editor

An Ottawa priest says his bishop has ordered him to stop promoting a Roman Catholic reform group that's calling for married and female priests.

Rev. Herman Falke said he was called in last week by Bishop Fred Colli to discuss a sermon he delivered Jan. 26 in which he endorsed some of the positions taken by Catholics of Vision, a group circulating a nationwide petition calling for reform in the church.

Falke believes the church ought to consider female priests and married clergy. He points out that the church already permits Ukrainian Catholic priests to marry, and some married former Anglican priests have been accepted as Roman Catholic priests.

He says the average age of Catholic priests in Canada is now over 60. "Somewhere, somehow there has to be some change in the church. Otherwise, people in the pews are going to lose heart," said Falke, a former missionary and well-known sculptor of religious art.

But at weekend services, Falke, 69,

Continued from page A1

Other parishioners are sending their petitions directly to Catholics of Vision.

He said that although a few parishioners in Osgoode were visibly disturbed by his original sermon, the majority appeared to favor many of the reforms suggested by Catholics of Vision, and all 100 copies of the group's vision statement were picked up at the back of the churches.

Guy Levac, a spokesman for the archdiocese of Ottawa, said Falke was not reprimanded and Colli was satisfied the priest genuinely misunderstood the archdiocese's decision in No-

apologized for upsetting some parishioners at his two parishes, St. John the Evangelist in Osgoode, and St. Brigid's, south of Manotick. "I told them I was not attacking in any way the authority of the church," he said Monday.

Falke said he will also obey Colli's order not to distribute any further Catholics of Vision literature through his parishes.

Falke said he has misgivings about parts of the Catholics of Vision statement, such as its call for freedom for theologians to publish and teach without censure. "That would produce absolute chaos in five years," he said, because it would confuse parishioners about what the church believes.

The Catholic church's stand is that women cannot become priests because Christ was a male and called only other men as his apostles. "To say the church can't reverse that is phoney," Falke said. "Christ and his apostles were all circumcised Galileans, too. Therefore, priests would all have to be circumcised Galileans."

Falke says "times have changed, and we've stepped into a different culture." He says he will be forwarding to Catholics of Vision the cheques and signed petitions handed to him by some of his parishioners.

PRIEST continued on page A2

vember to ban distribution of Catholics of Vision materials in local parishes. However, he said Colli will be discussing the Catholics of Vision petition today with Archbishop Marcel Gervais, Colli's superior. Colli is responsible for anglophone parishes in the diocese of Ottawa.

Saundra Glynn, national spokeswoman for Catholics of Vision, said it is sad that priests can't follow their conscience and promote discussion of issues like the need for lay input into Catholic sexual teachings and a reversal of the ban on communion for divorced and remarried Catholics.

"Every time they (the bishops) speak out against us, it helps our cause," she said.

More than 800 volunteers across

Canada began distributing petitions for Catholics of Vision on Jan. 6, and hope to collect thousands of signatures by May. Their efforts were sparked by a 1995 protest by Austrian and German Catholics, who collected 2.5 million signatures calling for open dialogue on contentious Catholic teachings. Similar petitions are now being circulated in the U.S., Britain, and several other countries.

To date, few of Canada's bishops have made any statement about Catholics of Vision. However, bishops in Saint John, N.B. and Vancouver have criticized the group as promoting dissension, and the archdioceses of Toronto and Ottawa are among those that have banned distribution of the petitions in their parishes.

Ottawa priest **Rev. Herman Falke says: 'Somewhere, somehow there has to be some change in the church.'**

Two couples and a spinster protested and left the parish, although three of them came back a few months later. Auxiliary Bishop Colli phoned me and tersely told me that I had to stop supporting that group.

The *Ottawa Citizen* had me on the front page with my photograph. The heading was: "Priest ordered to stop urging reform", with an article basically quoting the gist of my sermon.

My Religious Superior panicked and over the phone ordered me to keep silent and no longer discuss the issues of "Catholics of Vision".

After that, I became a nice, quiet priest, just sticking to my job, not interested in making waves. Anyway, soon after that I eagerly got involved in a big art project for a school, so that my mind was far away from Church squabbles.

The My Lai massacre

Throughout the post WWII period of 80 years by now the Americans, sometimes aided by Canadians and other Allies, waged wars around the fringe of Asia from Korea over Vietnam and Afghanistan to the Middle East, always basically to curb the threat of Communism. Most of these local wars bogged down into endless stalemates, notably the war in Vietnam. One episode became notoriously infamous as it was reported and even photographed by American news media: The My Lai Massacre.

In the 1970's in the exasperation of being hopelessly stuck in the jungles of Vietnam, a few American soldiers lost their cool, and massacred a small village, women and children mainly. World opinion was outraged, and rightly so. This disaster contributed to the Anti-Vietnam movement in the U.S.A. and around the world. In my painting from the mid 1970's I intersperse four happenings.

- Part of the actual massacre as it was photographed and appeared in Time Magazine.
- Part of the American G.I.s as checking the bodies and their huts.
- Part of the local nightlife, a continuation of the injury imposed on the Vietnamese
- Part of the crucifixion that somehow may bring a salvific solution to human folly.

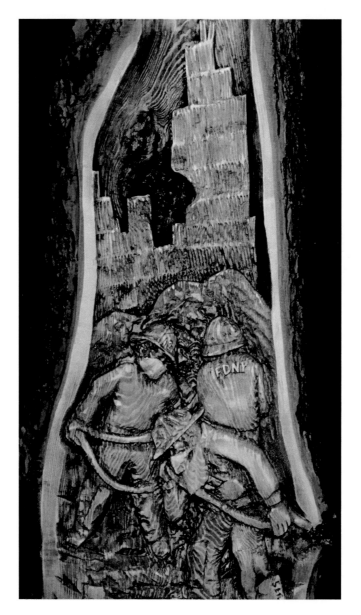

9/11 with NYFD

Narrow door

My parish ministry remained traditional, and not involved with city problems of drugs and homelessness. The four parishes I had in succession from when I return from Uganda to Canada in 1974 were all fairly well to-do suburban or rural parishes. We supported outreach programs, soup kitchens and shelters from a distance with regular financial support and Christmas actions. But for the rest I stuck to what I should call a "bourgeoisie ministry", functional, but far from ideal or virtuous. I was basically sacramental, and social. Father was always invited to wedding anniversaries, and had to say the official prayer at the Canadian Legion annually. The greying of the priests and their increasing shortage made this situation more and more the norm. I have no reason to apologize for that. I was sent by my Superiors specifically to teach music and art at secondary level. I trained for that and was good at it; I was never trained for any other career.

As the African saying goes: don't blame a brick for not being a wall. "Good Shepherd" and all that.

All such atrocities provoked repercussions. It had become a clash of ideologies, capitalism against a strange combination of fanatic Islam, nationalism and communism. Bin Laden threatened with retaliation not just against the U.S.A., but also Canada and other participants. American aggression stirred up nationalism and religious sentiments of revenge for Allah. With their advances in modern technology and their newly gained wealth from oil revenues, they showed their capacity to destroy any strategic hotspot in the U.S.A. The date, September 11, 2001, now known as 9/11 is forever graven on our memory. Four passenger jets taking off within 15 minutes of one another from three East Coast airports, were transformed by hijackers into fuel-laden missiles. Two pierced the World Trade Center towers, minutes apart, causing their collapse. Another pierced the Pentagon, and a fourth one, probably meant for the White House or Capitol was prevented by action of passengers and crash in a field in Pennsylvania. But forever the sense of immunity that North Americans had from being protected by three oceans, ended on 9/11.

I surprised myself when near the end of that month of September, 2001, I found inspiration to do my first 9/11 sculpture. What motivated me was the positive photograph on the cover of Time magazine showing three men from New York Fire Department working on the rubble of the World Trade Center to douse the fire and keep the ashes down. That positive gesture set me off.

An American visitor immediately took it home to Arizona while I was already mulling over a second version, this time more organized and more subtle in thought I selected a most suitable elongated endpiece of white pine that resembled a chimney and then carved the remains of the steel frame down to the rubble below. There I kept the main space for a Pieta not unlike Michelangelo's famous Pieta. Her sorrow in holding the body of Jesus for the last time coincides with the rubble behind her that holds the remains of hundreds of the victims of 9/11 including some of the fire fighters.

I realized the irony of the combination.

In the early 1950's Michelangelo's Pietà was transported for the first and only time outside of Italy to Manhattan Island N.Y. to make the centerpiece of the Vatican pavilion at the World Trade Fair.

9/11 with Pietà

When I had completed this carving and showed it to my Community in Ottawa, the Superior said: "This piece should remain here in the Community." It is still there in our dining room.

CHAPTER 7: MY ART REFLECTING CRISES OF THE TIME

9/11 with Guernica

My third version of the 9/11 sculpture is a combination of the contorted steel frame of the World Trade Fair with Picasso's "Guernica" in the foreground.

During the 1936-9 Spanish Civil War General Franco gladly accepted Hitler's offer to help by bombing the royalist stronghold of Guernica to ruins. In vain, people and animals are raising their arms and heads to heaven. Like Picasso I used newspapers with the actual reports printed on them Picasso's very long "Guernica" painting hung for many years in N.Y.s Museum of Modern Art, because Picasso did not allow the painting to go to Spain as long as General Franco was alive.

9/11 was a deep crisis that could have led to the destruction of cities or infrastructures in N. America and the Middle East. Cooler heads prevailed, and Bin Laden was surrepticiously taken out without any collateral damage.

As far as I am concerned, I was happy that I quickly followed up my early inspirations in creating positive and meaningful reactions to this dangerous crisis.

If I may boast, nowhere have I seen any such fortunate reactions in art to 9/11.

The steady process of creative art has protected me from loneliness and boredom, as Christmas cards and telephone calls demonstrate many elderly friends suffer from, right into my 90's.

That process involves that your mind and body are constantly engaged. Complex sculptures portraying human interaction are very suitable for that. Almost day and night you are mulling over in your mind how you should go about solving technical problems with wood or composition. Sometimes you have to stimulate that thinking process intentionally to keep it going, just as older people must continue to do some daily physical exercises in order to keep the muscles workable. In this Covid-19 crisis of our time I had the fortune of living in a supportive Religious Community with six other slightly younger confreres who were happy to do the shopping and cooking. I feel blest and grateful, and never lonely. I am providing two illustrations of what projects I am tackling in 2021 to keep boredom at bay and my mind sharp.

Here is a recent photograph of me holding up a large white-pine sculpture of some choristers and dancers from Florence around 1490. (i.e. before Columbus). I would never have tackled such a complex piece if there had not been a need for keeping myself occupied for over two months.

The other example is a version of the soup-kitchen line-up. I did this version in 2020 and expanded the number of lonely people. I spent an extra week on carving the second row of the line-up in the back, so deep that I cut through the back five times. The stack of soup bowls and the volunteer serving form a proper focus to the line-up.

Another crisis of our time has already been touched in connection with the two versions of the soup kitchen line-up.

Soup kitchen line-up

City life and individualism, the prevailing public opinion in North America that holds that the individual has certain rights with which nobody else not even the state should interfere, have brought about an increasing amount of loneliness that many people are finding themselves incapable of coping with. Rural or village life had largely kept loneliness at bay till the industrial age attracted people in droves into city life.

Mental illnesses and suicides were claiming their victims.

I reflect on these problems in the selection of any topics in art. Such pieces may not have been popular, if for financial reasons you were compelled to comply with the wishes and demands of the market, but they were handled by me nonetheless, because I was not under such restrictions.

In spite of cell phones and instant messaging, we modern people suffer the pain of loneliness and yearning for meaningful connection. Creative artists are exposing this frequently in novels, songs and paintings. How do we deal with this pain?

The bulk of our modern rock music provides a temporal shield to drown out the pain of our loneliness by booming rhythms and clanging guitars. Besides, the writhing lead singers scream into their mikes, and drown out every private thinking and emotion. It is as if the audience are on drugs and let go of themselves briefly.

The danger is that if we do not deal with loneliness, it may lead us to become hardened and desensitized persons, continuously searching for more and higher kicks. Lonely people cruising the nightspots and ending up in bad company with those whom they hope to alleviate their loneliness. "Ten Solitudes" bunches together in the compact space around a kitchen table a number of dissatisfactions in ordinary life: hiding behind a newspaper, absorbed in a toy or TV program or hairdo, an undefined feeling of emptiness, an outreach for anyone outside by phone.

Loneliness

Lost in the crowd

Everybody needs meaningful interaction with fellow human beings. When that is lacking, a sense of isolation or even alienation may occur. During previous centuries when nearly all people were still living in agricultural villages and small garrison and commercial towns, a steady interaction between people was normal. The industrial revolution and consequent urbanization changed this dramatically. The number of people in today's industrialized Western nations that have lost any sense of direction in life is increasing by the year. This loss is aggravated by the decline of authority that the Church used to have.

When the American painter, Geoffrey Tooker (1920-2011) created his "Subway" painting in 1950, he did not intend it as a protest, bur as an honest expression of his social concern. He wanted to express in art how he felt about the problem of urban isolation in his day.

There are different ways in art to show isolation. In "Subway", Tooker employs two devices. He makes people look away from each other, and he boxes each individual in, as in the telephone cells to the left and in the staircases.

For a while I hesitated to include in this book my version of Tooker's "Subway", because I borrowed so heavily from the original that I felt like a thief. But finally I gave in because that painting caught precisely that feeling of modern individualism and isolation that I hoped to catch in my art.
My irregular slab of wood gave me the opportunity to "do my own thing", especially in the right wing, where I introduce a touch of relief in the form of a young boy who thinks he sees the man of the $500 reward on the poster. The overhead concrete structure I formed into an empty crucifix to suggest the burden of urban life.

Picasso Centennial, Togo; "a Mirror Image"

In this painting-sculpture of a postage stamp celebrating the centennial of Picasso's birth, I was struck by Picasso's frankly facing the ravages of old age. He leaves it up to us to draw our own conclusions.

Critically looking at ourselves in a mirror can be a thoughtful exercise. What kind of a judgement should we make?

Do we think we see elegance, charm, smugness? Or do we unmask more humbling aspects?

The young woman in the left half of Picasso's painting on the postage stamp appears to search for the truth in her mirror image. Her face has lost its soft roundness, her breasts have sagged and her belly has severe folds like deep chicken scratches. No wonder there is a large orange tear trickling down her heated cheeks.

The magic touch of the artist is that instead of a reversed reflection, there is a poetic prophecy of the ravages of years to come. It is like using the device of a time machine in order to get a glimpse of what is to come. In Christian terms we are to look even beyond the inevitable decline of all flesh, to the Maranatha. As Jesus reassures Martha, "Whoever believes in me will live, even though he dies". (Jn. 11:25)

Narcissus

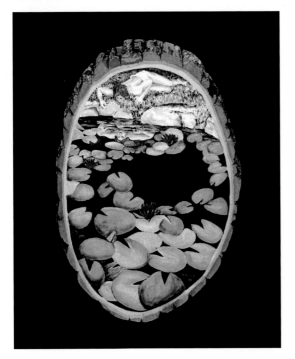

At our retreat house near Toronto there was an attractive pond with waterlilies and goldfish. I didn't wait long before painting it. Then, in order to give it a human connection, I included at the top the scene of Narcissus from Greek mythology who was looking into the deep dark to admire his own beauty (that was before modern mercury mirrors). His staring became so intense that he fell in and drowned.

Hey, you shouldn't fall in love with yourself! Remember, I only meant this painting to reflect the beauty of the pond. The frog in the foreground thinks I'm right.

What to do?

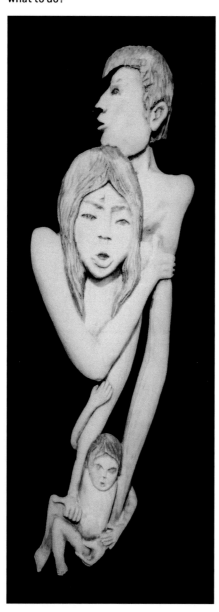

Sometimes people are simply lost. Firm teaching on moral values has largely disappeared. The vast majority of the young people are unable to even name the Ten Commandments, let alone keep them. Many also just step into marriage for the joy of sex without a clue how to raise their children. That's what I am suggesting in the sculpture of the young couple holding their baby far away. ("Any clean diaper around, dear?")

———

Almost 40 years ago I hesitated to bring this ceramic sculpture of my first "Earth Mother" to a church exhibition, because a priest had looked at it and had said," You shouldn't bring a sculpture like that to our church. It's a pagan goddess!"

I've learned to see the symbolical significance of portraying care for the world around us in depicting an earth mother, a creative force that sustains our universe. That old-fashioned priest had steered me into the opposite direction towards positive ecological concern. I've done six large "Earth Mother" woodcarvings. The first one was eagerly picked up at an Anglican Church exhibition by an Anglican elder from an Indian Reserve near Maniwaki As the two versions featured here show each one is quite unique, but all demonstrate the care for, from the top to bottom, birds, wind and rain, the ploughed earth, and the forests and native animals of North America, including also the fish and leaves at the bottom.

Indian Earth Mother
(Ceramic, 1983)

Is it an image gone forever to see the earth as a caring mother? Certainly our natives up north who are told not to eat the fish in the rivers nor to drink the water, must be wondering why the Christian clergy looked down upon their Earth Mother as an evil spirit.

Two parish mothers

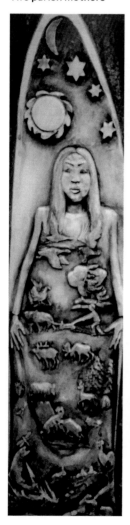 

But even large areas of tropical countries can no longer see the earth as a benign source of well-being. Poor sanitation, rapid urbanization and severe deforestation deplete and contaminate water sources at an alarming rate. The well water makes people sick and often leaves them suffering from parasites, diarrhea and intestinal illnesses. We are becoming aware of the whole of nature carrying cancer-producing pollutants in air, water, and chemical by-products in our foods. We pay a heavy price for our technical advances and mass industrial products.

Still, we have to continue living today and tomorrow, let alone fifty years from now. While species of animals continue to disappear, while the world's forests dwindle, while the ozone protection against UV rays fades, we individuals may have to be content with tackling a manageable project within our own community such as a garbage dump that may be a breeding ground for rats and lice that carry infectious diseases. Another good project would be the promotion of composting, recycling and organic gardening.

CHAPTER 7: MY ART REFLECTING CRISES OF THE TIME

Meanwhile the global destruction of our living conditions is creeping up on us, paper cup after paper cup, plastic drinking straw after plastic straw, chewing gum wad after chewing gum wad. Each single bit is harmless, but billions each week becomes destructive. The global carbon emission from fossil-fuel burning creates heat waves that cause all glaciers to collapse. By the end of this century the sea level will have risen over a meter and cause whole islands to disappear. Climatic change influences severe weather by causing longer droughts and higher temperatures in some regions and more intense deluges in others.

My reactions as an artist to this long-term crisis to our survival has been moderate thus far. I've approached the ecological threat to our planet by encouraging proper care for our surroundings as symbolically inspired by "Mother Earth". Painting on this subject automatically turned in the direction of surrealism which I usually avoid because of the negative reaction of most people around me to off-beat creations.

In the painting "Creator and Creation destroyed", I am expressing my conviction that we are offending Christ, or God, when we participate in letting God's creation fall to pieces. It is like participating in the crucifixion of Christ even without raising a hand.

Creator and creation destroyed (1990)

Lower Yonge Street

There is another painting where I expressed the same feeling that our failure to curb our sexual excesses will continue our complicity in the Passion of Christ in our time, or in other terms, we slow down the process of our evolution.

Lower Yonge Street in Toronto is a well-known fleshpot. Juxtaposed to that I painted that moment in the Passion story where the three condemned criminals have just been nailed to the side beam, and are waiting to be hoisted up. Above their heads, on parking meters, are the inscriptions of their crimes: child molester, rapist, claiming kingship. Mother Mary and the Apostle John are trying to support each other, while other spectators find it difficult to take it all in.

Further explanation would be merely personal speculation. We are like most of the spectators in the foreground: in our time when our society has become lax in allowing pornography, teenage sex, and marriage infidelity, we find it difficult to come to terms with some of our weaknesses of the flesh.

Especially when I am confronted with a crisis that I find unmanageable, I tend to resort to surrealism where I force together incongruous images that somehow produce a concept that could not be expressed in a normal way.

CHAPTER 7: MY ART REFLECTING CRISES OF THE TIME

When there is a thunderstorm approaching we see far away flashings of lightning, followed several seconds later by rumbling of thunder. As children we used to count slowly from the moment we saw lightning, because eight seconds till thunder meant that the storm was still 8 x 300=2.400 meters away.

The speed of sight is so much faster than the speed of sound, namely hundreds of times faster.

I used this discrepancy in my painting "Tomorrow?" The young woman is enjoying the pleasures of a luxurious life on a Caribbean beach at the very moment that an atomic bomb hits Miami, Florida, 80 miles away.

Will the fall-out reach her? How many seconds from now? Will there be a tomorrow?

Tomorrow…?

You are here (1st version)

A final and most suitable crisis I felt called to respond to artistically was the dawning awareness of a gradual evolution of a human intelligence and a subsequent parallel evolution of religion.

A few million years ago some humanoid chimps in East Africa jumped down from their trees and formed groupings to achieve safety and successful hunting, and later on agriculture. Finally only about 6-7000 years ago, around the Nile and Asiatic rivers near deserts, they developed different sets of writing as well as systems of moral behaviour. These became what we nowadays categorize as Buddhism, Confucianism, and Judaism. A few offshoots of these later became self-assured, aggressive factions, notably Roman Catholics, Muslims, and Jehovah Witnesses, each claiming that they alone had the Truth, and all the others were wrong and headed for eternal damnation.

In my lifetime, and specifically since Vatican II in the 1960's there has been a reluctant acknowledgment from the Hierarchy and an enthusiastic welcome from liberal-minded Catholics that the Church must adapt to the times and not remain rooted in the Middle Ages. Our advanced understanding of new science (like the earth is travelling around the sun, and not the other way around) must lead to advancing religious understanding. What is old deserves to be challenged.

My sculpture "you are here" suggests that progress in the human evolutionary process is a gradual one, thousands upon thousands of years. As I usually do when I am dealing with an exciting theme, I made a second, longer version which included individuals who were handling tools or weapons, put on clothes, but ultimately got back into the trees to become monkeys again.

A collector of my art who lives on the Caribbean island of St. Vincent bought this second version but expressed a desire for a third version which retains a progressive line into an astronaut preparing for a trip into outer space. Here it is, but Covid-19 has thus far prevented my friend from collecting it.

You are here (3rd version)

If a religious institution, if a Church intends to have a future, it must be open to accept new scientific developments. Jesus himself declared that the improvements he hoped to bring about in Judaic practices was like pouring "new wine into new skins"

By now the younger half of the Catholics in North America and Europe have already left the Church. At present it is the seniors who are agonizing over leaving an institute that clings to an irrelevant past and intends to remain an old wine skin. Actually it is a logical step in the evolutionary process: whatever bogs down or stagnates will face extinction. The new wine will burst the old skins.

All this revolutionary development in thinking disturbed me, while at the same time it was too far above my head to make me throw my hat into the ring and join the fight. I was resigned to leave that to experts and read about it after the dust had settled.

My art was only collaterally affected by it as in my humorous speculations on evolution in "You are here".

However, there was one aspect of the evolution speculation that caught my specific attention. One new scientific discovery was the much larger size of the solar system and the surrounding Cosmos. There are literally billions of stars with billions of planets around them. It is becoming highly likely that there exist thousands of planets where human life like ours, or unlike ours, exists. Then following our familiar way of thinking, there could have taken place another God-directed creation, even without things going partly wrong as our Bible suggests it did on our planet. God said to Adam: "you will be punished for your disobedience. The ground will be under a curse. You will have to work hard all your life and sweat to make the soil produce anything." Gen 3:17

Today as we are struggling to come to terms with an apparently infinite and random universe we may also have to change our worn out conceptions of God and soul and guilt and original sin and what not, knowing from experience that our institutional church will continue to dawdle on these touchy issues for centuries as it did with Galileo Galilei and his rejection of the idea that the Sun moves around the Earth each 24 hours. Scientific facts will win out, even if it takes centuries.

My relatively recent awareness of an infinitely larger cosmos has made it easier for me to reject the Church notion of a geocentric universe that even shapes God into an earth satellite, a "Big Brother's eye in the sky".

I am getting at peace with the idea that I am like one grain of sand on a long beach that holds the ocean at bay.

A grain of sand by itself is insignificant, and yet it is meaningful and functional in a wider scheme of things Likewise in the larger scheme of evolutionary development, my remaining faithful adherence to Christian practices, as long as no better forms present themselves, is still meaningful. It gives me satisfaction and contentment.

CHAPTER 7: MY ART REFLECTING CRISES OF THE TIME

Incarnation elsewhere
(1996)

CHAPTER 8
THE GOLDEN YEARS

Stages in life
(White pine, 44"x20", 2000)

Mae West said it best, "You only live once, but if you do it right, once is enough."
Life has its natural rhythms of play and earnest work, carefree enjoyment and duty bound respon-
sibility. It's this whole package that turns
life into a worth-while celebration. Each
stage has its charm, though the pains and
aches of old age may make you wonder
how "charming" that stage is. But at least
it should be the appropriate time to recol-
lect in tranquility.

Quadruple self-portrait

I doubt if Norman Rockwell at age 66
was at a tall serious when he painted his
triple self- portrait for the cover of *Saturday Evening Post* in Feb, 1960. Neither was
I at the age of 62, when I imitated Norman
Rockwell in my own way.

I was intrigued when the Toronto Department of Education was offering a course in self-portrait painting directed by a young Chinese lady. Eleven signed up for this strange course of 12 weeks.

That was September 1989, and I started with an acrylic sketch of myself modelling in clay the statue of Adam and Eve. (See Chapter Five.) In the final painting on canvas, that sketch underneath my easel made it a quadruple self-portrait.

Critics in my studio (White pine, 44"x23", 2002)

I reduced Rockwell's busy row of models to just one more, nutty Dutchman, Vincent van Gogh, an artist who used the self-portrait very seriously to express his tortured soul. That's far away from my intentions.

For me it was a question of exercise, and fun. Nor was my sculpture "Critical visitors in my studio" an honest portrayal of genuine feelings of painful rejection and misunderstanding. In the 50 years of my art career I have not received any negative criticism, except one or two rumblings of disapproval from two old-fashioned clergymen. (I put a Roman collar on the third protester.)

No, I meant this sculpture to be contrived, — a joke at my expense, just as my "quadruple self-portrait" was.

It is by sheer accident that I end up my major art week with two pleasant fakes. How about that? Freud, help us out!

My interest in Canadian politics has diminished drastically as of late. At present I could not name more than one minister in Prime Minister Trudeau's Cabinet. Our political scandals and mismanagements are trivial in comparison with the recent disastrous four years under Trump just south of us. However, once in a while something exciting happens even in placid Canada that seems designed to wake me up.

Such was the case with the G8 summit in 2002.

On a dull day in 2002, the G8 summit was held in Ottawa. To explain several photos taken from behind, the Ottawa Citizen wrote. "As protests wound down, a group of about ten, mostly men, stripped naked, and sparked up their remaining marijuana joints and dangled their bodies before the wet, tired crowd." The financial progress of the world's richest nations was again assured for another year.

G8 Summit '02
(White pine, 2002)

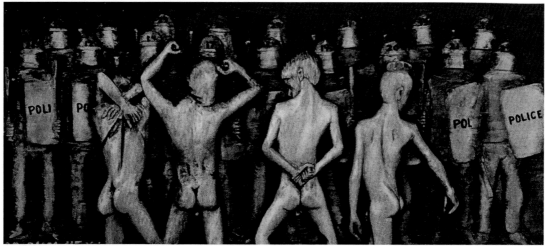

White House toilet

The four years of Donald Trump's Presidency from 2016 till 2020 reminded me of the five years I lived as a teenager through the dictatorship of Hitler from 1940 till 1945. Both men dealt out packs of lies and misinformation. Fortunately Trump did not resort to mass executions, but limited himself to defamation and dismissals. Whoever refuses to be a yes-man is tossed out like garbage.

The impact of Trump on my life was not deep enough to call it a crisis. Actually his erratic shenanigans became so ridiculous that they provided a daily entertainment. Our dinnertime expanded as we exchanged our hilarious reactions.

Our S.C.J. Communities in the U.S.A. reacted quite differently. The division of opinions became so painfully sharp that a few Communities almost fell apart. Some confreres simply overlooked Trump's glaring faults for the fact that he firmly advocated Respect for Life and blocked abortion.

Trump looking in the mirror

It became an unwritten house rule in our American Communities that during mealtimes Trump was not to be discussed. I presume that the same clash occurred in many households throughout the U.S.A., while Trump managed to keep playing the Americans for suckers with his fascist rhetoric.

On my way to a solo exhibition I had near Green Bay, Wisconsin, I discovered in Espanola on the north shore of Georgian Bay a sawmill operator who made useful slabs of wood, one inch thick. He used mainly poplar trees that were cut down in late Fall or Winter (so that the bark remained firmly attached to the wood) and saved them in diagonal slabs for maximum display space. Then he would sand them and store them separately for drying. He made a good living from them by selling them all over North America as boards to display stuffed trophy fish or birds.

Since 2004 I've bought dozens of them and used them especially for landscape paintings. They are light-weight and require no framing. I have selected two Quebec-inspired subjects, and five others that deal with special topics.

Of some 30 Quebec scenes I did on these oval slabs, this one proved to be the most popular. I did it three times and have no copy of it myself at present. People around here seem to identify quite easily with such a simple setting of one or two cabins on open water.

Charlevoix (after works by Vladimir Horik)

After "At Mass, Baie St. Paul" 1871-1953

One of my hobbies is collecting wild edible mushrooms. I learned this from my Mother, 85 years ago... and I'm still alive. My field guide on wild mushrooms in Quebec unexpectedly informed me that a certain large, delightful mushroom is commonly found around churches in the Gaspé peninsula. Pastors around the Gaspe may be suspected of delivering long sermons. No wonder that the mushroom is best known as "horse mushroom".

Northern Lights

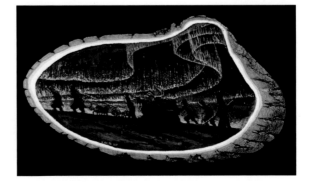

I let my sawmill friend from Espanola know that I was eager to receive from him oval slabs that were irregular in shape. I love to improvise around such irregularities, as I do here with the swirls of the Northern Lights overhead of the travelling Inuit with only a sliver of daylight.

Pee Wee Hockey brawl

Pee Wee hockey is controlled by adults both on the ice and from the visitor's gallery. Again, I happily improvised with the irregular shape of the slab.

Hibbs Cove, Newfoundland

I once saw a painting of Hibbs Cove, Newfoundland done by a visiting artist from Lithuania I thought it really captured the local landscape with a typical human activity: cleaning fish. My cut-off oval slab represents the cold emptiness of the North Atlantic.

San Gimignano, Tuscany, land of Chianti wine and Lacrima Christi

Tuscany around Florence is blest with good soil and a mild Mediterranean climate, ideal to grow olives, oranges, and of course grapes to produce wines. Some successful producers of these crops started competing with each other in displaying their wealth and prominence by building useless high towers. These are still a tourist attraction.

Paul Tex Lecor, "La fille a Louis, Port-Daniel, Gaspe" 1985

A New Brunswick setting with a girl bringing a lunch to two fisherman.

At this late stage of my life it's getting time to shut up and let the new generation have the word. From them will come a new vision of God, humanity and the Church. All that remains to be done by me is to summarize my main achievements and main failures.

My main failure has been that I never had a promoter, a "dealer" who for a percentage would take care of my output and promote it in the right places. That kind of commercial thinking never took hold of me.

In the 1950's and 1960's I lived in a semi-monastic atmosphere that frowned on commercial success and worldly involvement. Moreover, my commitment to the Church caused me to be moved around from place to place. As a result my prolific output combined with my several moves forced me into giant giveaways, donations for worthy causes, door prizes etc. These in turn undermined my natural market.

A second failure is related to the first. I was an easy victim for hard-pressed art galleries that were willing to sell my work for a commission of 40% or so. Of the six galleries that I tried that way, occasionally, three downright cheated me, sold my sculptures, and never paid me: one in Halifax, one in Ottawa, and one in Winnipeg. The one in Ottawa went bankrupt because the owner was an alcoholic, who had a chaotic bookkeeping system. But I heard that he used my lack of business savvy as his sales pitch: 'the artist is a priest belonging to a Religious Society. He doesn't know the value of money. That's why my price is so reasonable.

The world of small galleries is pretty hard-nosed, and an unsuitable world for a "softie" like me. Besides, I was never short of money as my teaching and Church ministry covered all my living expenses so that my sales of art simply provided surplus cash. The rate of the three delinquent galleries must have smelled that. If starving artists become the best artists, I never had a chance to be the best.

I consider my five solo exhibitions and my seven publications of art books minor successes. They were the normal signposts in the career of any self-respecting artist. But what I consider my main achievement was the laborious creation of *"And This is what He Taught"*, a 260-page meditation book on the most inspiring biblical events, from Genesis to the Apocalypse. It has 111 meditations each one accompanied by one of my sculptures. It was published in 2011 in English, French, and Dutch editions. The main reason why I succeeded in this major undertaking was international collaborations, one with an American Franciscan Nun, and the other with a Dutch Priest. Holy company!

Sister Irene Zimmerman, OSF, was a published poet. At my first exhibition of spiritual sculptures in a retreat house in Wisconsin. I found a lovely poem pinned underneath one of my sculptures, while I didn't know her. Three years later we had a joint exhibition of our sculptures and poetry, side by side, in that Wisconsin gallery. A dozen of my sculptures there, were the direct result of that collaboration, and three of her newly published poems were inspired by my sculptures.

Sarah compelling Abraham to cast out Hagar, her slave girl
(Cedar, 17"x15", 2002)

The other international collaboration was with Fr Piet Schellens, who happened to be a Scripture scholar. He took a liking to my work and asked me to provide him with 60 specific sculptures for a publication he had in mind. This was repeated two and again four years later. As a result we were covering more and more biblical ground together. This helped me greatly to finally put it all together in my Swan Song, *"And This is what He Taught."*

These two collaborators, each in turn, challenged me to come up with some original points of view on a specific bible story. I hereby show two of their contributions. Both happen to deal with Abraham, the Father of our Jewish, Christian, and Islam faith.

Abraham and the three visitors
(White pine, 24"x14", 2001)

The one story deals with Abraham's hospitality under his oak tree, while his wife Sarah listens in. The other story tells how old Abraham is caught between his two squabbling wives.

I must confess that during the last few years my steady routine of woodcarving every complete morning was somewhat artificial. I intended it to keep mind and body active, and I think I succeeded. I challenged myself with attempting some really complicated themes such as a tall sculpture that I am holding in the last photo, although the pandemic kept all visitors away and destroyed the market for art.

I could do that in the security of a supportive Religious Community. And thanks to God for my life-long physical and mental health!

Looking back over my life I see that it could easily have turned into an average dull life, if it hadn't been perked up by those two international collaborations, and even earlier and more so by two fortunate moves I made, the first one from Holland to Canada, and the second to Uganda for some enlightening years.

The move from Holland to Canada put me into a sink-or-swim situation. Suddenly I had to improvise and make decisions on my own, rather than fall into a slot that was already determined by others before me. In Canada it proved easier to choose directions and opportunities that happened to come my way. Aside from doing my expected duties of teaching and supplying priestly work, I could concentrate on becoming on an artist against all odds.

When the mid 1960's finally brought to the surface a deep crisis in the Church, which to me came in the form of evidence that my teaching in a Seminary was becoming pointless and a waste of time in the best part of my life, I searched and found a rewarding escape in Uganda. What I learned and gained there could never be taken away from me by the set-back of Idi Amin's cruel dictatorship.

In life, happy events are interwoven with set-backs. One can just let life pass you by, or one can use it as a learning experience, or even celebrate it in art, music, drama.

Masks of comedy and tragedy
(White pine, 20"x9.5", 1997)

As the Good Book states in Psalm 90: "Our lifespan is seventy years, or eighty for the strong. Yet mostly they bring us trouble and sorrow."

Then the Psalmist ends with a prayerful wish: "Make us come to terms with that relative shortness of our life, so that we may gain wisdom of heart."

I am content: I loved my life in spite of my introverted hesitation of shouting out that happiness. I trust that my paintings and sculptures may do the shouting for me.